Making Sense of Developmentally and Culturally Appropriate Practice (DCAP) in Early Childhood Education

Rethinking Childhood

Joe L. Kincheloe and Janice A. Jipson
General Editors

Vol. 6

PETER LANG
New York • Washington, D.C./Baltimore • Boston
Bern • Frankfurt am Main • Berlin • Vienna • Paris

Eunsook Hyun

Making Sense of Developmentally and Culturally Appropriate Practice (DCAP) in Early Childhood Education

PETER LANG
New York • Washington, D.C./Baltimore • Boston
Bern • Frankfurt am Main • Berlin • Vienna • Paris

Library of Congress Cataloging-in-Publication Data

Hyun, Eunsook.
Making sense of developmentally and culturally appropriate
practice (DCAP) in early childhood education / Eunsook Hyun.
p. cm. — (Rethinking childhood; 6)
Includes bibliographical references (p.   ) and index.
1. Early childhood education—United States. 2. Child development—United States.
3. Multicultural education—United States. I. Title. II. Series:
Rethinking childhood; v. 6.
LB1139.25.H97 372.21—dc21 97–12508
ISBN 0-8204-3765-4
ISSN 1086-7155

Die Deutsche Bibliothek-CIP-Einheitsaufnahme

Hyun, Eunsook:
Making sense of developmentally and culturally appropriate practice (DCAP)
in early childhood education / Eunsook Hyun. –New York; Washington, D.C./Baltimore;
Boston; Bern; Frankfurt am Main; Berlin; Vienna; Paris: Lang.
(Rethinking childhood; 6)
ISBN 0-8204-3765-4

Cover design by James F. Brisson.

The paper in this book meets the guidelines for permanence and durability
of the Committee on Production Guidelines for Book Longevity
of the Council of Library Resources.

∞

© 1998 Peter Lang Publishing, Inc., New York

Printed in the United States of America.

This book is dedicated to Yevin

Acknowledgments

I am indebted to many people at the Pennsylvania State University for their help in the completion of this book. The first expression of my deep appreciation goes to James Van Horn, professor of rural sociology. Without his insights that he shared with me, it would have been impossible for me to acknowledge what is the true meaning of developmentally and culturally appropriate practice. Uncovering unknown human knowledge requires a high level of intellectual challenge and risk taking as well as intellectual excitement. Dan Marshall, professor of education, moved me into a new way of exploring and constructing knowledge. James Nolan introduced me a very important intellectual function "reflectivity" in teachers' cognition. It was the most important tool that I depended upon during my research for this book. All these pieces of intellectual influences came into one completed puzzle when I met Nancy Fichtman Dana. She was the first person who introduced me how to explore the world from a qualitative researcher's point of view. Qualitative paradigm has led me to see, feel, taste, listen, and smell the power of human culture that we have created, particularly in many forms of teaching and learning contexts. My first deepest appreciation goes to these people that I encountered at Penn State.

Without my two special students Ana and Carrie, my theoretical teacher preparation model for developmentally and culturally appropriate practices wouldn't have become a lived practice. Their strong commitment to bring an early childhood education that is for all was the driving force for me to articulate this book. With these two prospective teachers' unconditional help the theory has transformed to practice.

In writing this book, I also received invaluable supports of many people whose contributions I wish to acknowledge. This book belongs to my son Yevin and my mother Soongil Lee. I remember their endless support, encouragement, and patients. Hazel Hunley was a good listener and emotional supporter in my previous work for this book. Her professional editing was highly appreciated in this work. My thanks also goes to Joe Kincheloe and Shirley Steinberg who were interested in and willing to publish my work. I would also like to appreciate Chris Myers and Jackie Pavlovic at Peter Lang for their assistance.

I would like to acknowledge the National Association for the Education of Young Children (NAEYC) for granting me permission to reprint part of the revised developmentally appropriate practice (DAP) position statement which appears on page 6 (Developmentally Appropriate Practice in early Childhood Programs, by Bredekamp & Copple, Copyright © 1997 by NAEYC. All rights reserved). The National Council for Accreditation of Teacher Education (NCATE), Approved Curriculum Guidelines that appears on pages xi - xii are also reprinted with the permission of NCATE (NCATE Approved Curriculum Guidelines, 1992, 1994, 1997. Washington, DC. Reprinted by permission NCATE. All right reserved). I also acknowledge the Association for Supervision and Curriculum Development (ASCD) for granting me permission to reprint my previous work co-authored with J. D. Marshall which appears on pages 75 - 92 (From *Journal of Curriculum and Supervision*: Hyun, Eunsook & Marshall, Dan, J. "Inquiry-Oriented Reflective Supervision for Developmentally and Culturally Appropriate Practice." Winter 1996. 11, 1: 127-144. Reprinted with permission of ASCD. Copyright © 1996 by ASCD. All right reserved). My last acknowledgment goes to the Association for Childhood Education International (ACEI). In Chapter 3, pages 42 - 52 is reprinted by ACEI granted permission (From *Journal of Research in Childhood Education*: Hyun, Eunsook & Marshall, Dan, J. "Theory of multiple/multiethnic perspective-taking ability for teachers' DCAP." 1997, *11* (2), 188-198. Copyright © 1997 by ACEI. All right reserved).

Table of Contents

Preface

Since 1979, U.S. teacher education programs have been expected to prepare teachers for "education that is multicultural education"--a significant task for initial teacher preparation (National Council for Accreditation of Teacher Education [NCATE], 1979, 1992, 1994, 1997). However, preparing teachers to develop the capability and sensitivity to respond well to the multiple/multiethnic perspectives of diverse learners has caused considerable controversy. Most teacher education programs exhibit limited procedures and practices in preparing teachers to be culturally sensitive and to use their discovery of multiculturalism as an inherent pedagogical resource (Baker, 1994; Cannella & Reiff, 1994; Fuller, 1992; Hinchey, 1994; Huberman, 1991; Marshall, 1994).

In addition, NCATE standards discuss the necessity of addressing Developmentally Appropriate Practice (DAP) (Bredekamp, 1987; Bredekamp & Copple, 1997) in conjunction with multicultural education in early childhood teacher education programs. DAP is an important philosophical framework and related pedagogical guideline in early childhood education that emphasizes age appropriateness, individual appropriateness, and social and cultural appropriateness when planning programs for young children. Regarding DAP and multicultural education, NCATE standards prepared by the National Association for the Education of Young Children (NAEYC) provide the following guidelines for early childhood teacher education programs:

> The curriculum prepares candidates to work effectively in a culturally diverse society...The curriculum provides candidates with integrated and interdisciplinary knowledge and understanding of child development from birth through age eight...Curriculum for teaching young children includes the following: Planning, implementing, and evaluating developmentally appropriate content and methodology... preparation for working in settings that include atypical children understanding the needs of developmentally diverse children...and

comprehension of cultural diversity and its implications. (NCATE, 1994, pp. 291-302)

...programs prepare early childhood professionals who...Apply knowledge of cultural and linguistic diversity and the significance of socio-cultural and political contexts for development and learning, and recognize that children are best understood in the contexts of family, culture, and societ...Demonstrate understanding of the interrelationships among cultures, language, and thought and the function of the home language in the development of young children...Affirm and respect culturally and linguistically diverse children, support home language preservation, and promote anti-bias approaches through the creation of learning environments and experiences...Demonstrate sensitivity to differences in family structures and social and cultural backgrounds...Demonstrate an understanding of the early childhood profession, its multiple historical, philosophical, and social foundations, and how these foundations influence current thought and practice. (NACTE, 1994, pp. 235-243 / 1997, pp. 272-284)

In response to these NCATE standards, teacher preparation programs have focused their efforts on educating prospective teachers and providing course work to prepare teachers for the culturally diverse children they will teach. However, schools and colleges of teacher education have neither aggressively nor consistently organized teacher education programs to prepare teachers who must function and teach in a diverse society (Baker, 1994; Dana, 1992; Fuller, 1992).

In early childhood education, the issue of culturally appropriate practice has inspired teacher educators to realize the needs of teacher preparation for both developmentally and culturally appropriate practice for early childhood education (Bowman, 1992, 1994). For these purposes early childhood teacher preparation for Developmentally *and Culturally* Appropriate Practice (DCAP) has been suggested (Hyun, 1996; Hyun & Dana, in press; Hyun & Marshall, 1996, 1997).

Teacher preparation for education that is multicultural is not simply about sensitizing teachers to race, gender, ethnicity, religion, diverse socioeconomic status, and sexual orientation. Rather, this preparation should help prospective teachers develop an understanding of themselves and their individual family and ethnic cultures so that they might realize how their individual histories, backgrounds, and ethnic family cultures make them different from (and similar to) others. An approach to teacher preparation that helps new teachers recognize the multiple/multiethnic perspectives employed by diverse learners becomes a matter of learning, valuing, and being willing to integrate learners' *many best ways* of making sense of their learning and their world within a multiethnic learning environment. This initial teacher preparation permits prospective teachers to make connections between these realizations and their instructional efforts by conducting and maintaining an equal, fair, and culturally congruent learning experience for *all* individual learners.

The main purpose of this book is to present process-oriented, reflective early childhood teacher preparation for DCAP to achieve education that is truly multicultural--for *all* individuals. DCAP relies upon critical pedagogy and attempts to add the extremely important cultural dimension and teachers' self-awareness and usage of the cultural dimension to the newly revised notion of developmentally appropriate practice (Bredekamp & Copple, 1997). This book is designed for early childhood teacher educators and graduate students who study early childhood curriculum and pedagogical issues. For undergraduates, this book can be infused into courses that deal with programs for young children, DAP, child's play and development, family and teacher relations, as well as field-based courses which have a supervision component. Currently, there is no textbook that either deals with the orientation of DCAP or gives an overall in-depth picture of DCAP teacher preparation. In addition, this book discusses early childhood education that is multicultural in a different context from other existing literature. It is hoped that this new literature will bring a new and a different era of understanding and promoting the true meaning of multiculturalism in early childhood education that emphasizes the individual's multiple/multiethnic perspective-taking.

The following chapters illustrate how the notion of DCAP teacher preparation interplays with the DAP framework in order for the early childhood teachers to provide an equal, fair, and culturally congruent learning experience for *all* children. In 1996, I presented a teacher preparation model in that regard which has multiple approaches. The following chapters describe in-depth procedures and empirical approaches to those that I described in the model.

Chapter 1 discusses the conceptual understanding and definition of appropriate practice in conjunction with differentiating DAP and DCAP. This chapter should be relevant to graduate curriculum courses and undergraduate courses that discuss the limits of DAP.

In early childhood education and developmental psychology, it has been understood that child development and play are inseparable human developmental phenomena. Yet, that notion needs to be readdressed in conjunction with culture, particularly with family and ethnic cultures. Culture shapes the nature of child's play and its subsequent developmental phenomena. Chapter 2 presents contemporary cross-cultural perspectives on child's play and attempts to revisit some of our preexisting knowledge of child's play, discuss its limits and critical aspects, and readdress the notion differently for DCAP teacher preparation. Chapter 2 should be relevant to courses that deal with child's play and human development and growth.

In process-oriented teacher preparation for developmentally and culturally appropriate practice, developing one's own multiple/multiethnic perspective-taking ability is the main key. In chapter 3, I discuss an autobiographical self-awareness approach in the development of multiple/multiethnic perspective-taking. This approach can be implemented in a course which has a field-based component in it or on-site workshop for in-service practitioners. It will enhance the preservice and the in-service development of reflective teaching and ongoing self-evaluation. This experience would be particularly effective in a field-based workshop with groups of preservice and in-service teachers with diverse levels of experience.

In addition, when the prospective teachers are in the initial stage of teacher education courses, this Chapter 3 should be relevant to courses that deal with human growth, change, and learning, particularly social cognitive development. This fairly new theory of multiple/multiethnic perspective-taking ability (Hyun & Marshall, 1997) is different from the theory of social perspective-taking (Selman, 1980) and Piaget's (1952) conventional theory of child's developmental perspective-taking in that it is directly related to teachers' social-cognitive pedagogical behavior. Thus this theory will affect their future professional practice for a pluralistic society.

In Chapter 4, I introduce implications of the theory of developing multiple/multiethnic perspective-taking for teachers' DCAP in conjunction with ways of studying culture and ethnicity. I strongly suggest that you use the ways of studying ethnic family cultures and the instructional approach in chapter 4 in any child development courses and courses on child's play and family relations. I would like to recommend especially that you use this approach at the beginning of such courses before the prospective teachers are exposed to "conventional" or "universal" orientation of child development, child's play, and parental involvement, so that the teacher's fundamental orientation to early childhood education will not be narrowed by concepts that are alleged to be race blind, ethnically blind, or culturally blind.

In my earlier work on DCAP teacher preparation for early childhood education, it has mentioned that in order to have successful early childhood teacher preparation for DCAP, we also need to provide inquiry-oriented reflective supervision for prospective teachers' formal field experiences (Hyun & Marshall, 1996). Such an approach focuses on helping them to become reflective practitioners who are both process- and outcome-oriented. Student teachers examine classroom phenomena from multiple perspectives and recognize how the decisions they make influence the learning that occurs. They look critically at the ethical bases of what happens in the classroom and determine how to extend practices that will affect all learners. Chapter 5 focuses on DCAP's integration within field experiences--student teaching experience and its supervision.

In 1995, my dissertation study was on exploring how prospective early childhood teachers make sense of DCAP in their first novice teaching experiences. Chapter 6 introduces the research contexts and qualitative methodological approach of that study using the supervision model developed in chapter 5. Chapter 7 discusses the results and implications of the research. This study serves as a point of departure for continued dialogue and discussion on how to prepare our future early childhood teachers to meet the needs of *all* children in a pluralistic society.

Chapter One

What Is Appropriate Practice?

Practice is a purposeful action and experience. Appropriate practice is a purposeful action and experience within a social context. In a social institution such as a school, teachers conventionally seem to be the initial agents of "appropriate practice" for learners' well-being. In this context, each teacher's appropriate practice reflects social values based on his/her own sociocultural backgrounds. The teacher translates those values into experiences for the individual learners. Once the teacher practices in a classroom with children who are from different sociocultural backgrounds than the teacher's, the teacher's appropriate practice should go beyond his/her own sociocultural backgrounds to incorporate the diverse sociocultural contexts, since these would be more responsible and relevant to the diverse young learners' growth and optimal learning experiences. Thus, appropriate practice contains an inherent dynamic of change, which is the nature of teachers' everyday practice.

Appropriate practice is purposeful action and experience that enables all learners to construct a knowledgeable, confident, positive self-identity and to develop multiple perspectives in understanding self, other, and diverse social phenomena--all of which are fundamental cognitive tools for their living. An appropriate practice responds positively to the individual's unique and different phases of growth, change, and learning styles. By doing so it enables all learners to discover their own fullest potential.

In a multiethnic and multicultural school culture, as in the United States, appropriate practice that responds to diverse learners' unique developmental and learning potentials is necessary and should be part of the basic awareness in teachers' everyday practice to ensure equal and fair teaching and learning experiences for all learners. The goal of appropriate practice is to provide optimal conditions in all aspects of individual learners' living in classrooms. Under optimal conditions, the learner is recognized as a unique individual who is free to express his/her own cultures, languages, ideas, feelings, questions, unique communication styles, learning styles, and problem-solving skills. In appropriate practice, the provided optimal conditions include physical environments as well as hidden environments that support one's own self-image and identity.

Providing the optimal conditions as appropriate practice leads individuals to be free to express their own uniqueness and capability, to share about themselves, and to challenge themselves to (re)discover their own potentials. The individual is free from "limits" that come from being labeled from a single perspective--second language speaker/learner, nonstandard English speaker; physically, ethnically, or racially different; physically disabled, learning disabled; special needs learner; single-parent child, child of gay or lesbian parents and so on. Instead, individual characteristics and the conditions of individual differences are recognized as parts of diverse human uniqueness. Appropriate practice perceives and supports the notion that individuals are unique in their own ways; their behavior, learning styles, communication styles, and problem-solving skills are derived from their own family culture, which supports individuals' self-identity. In such an environment, all individuals realize the existence of human diversity and multiple perspectives in learning and development, which are multidirectional and nonlinear.

How do teachers achieve a purposeful action? What is the process of teachers making appropriate practices? One answer is that such teachers began to question the traditional notion of development which is based on a single linear paradigm that focuses on only one way of looking at human growth and changes; at a certain age one can do certain things or not, and it always ends with a last stage of development as the highest level. Thus, within this traditional paradigm, our vision of human development stays within a limit and cannot go beyond the "highest level": the "group orientation," or different ways of understanding and supporting diverse human developmental growth and changes. The teachers who develop appropriate practice, however, deconstruct their perception of the conventional human development and learning and reconstruct it as continuous individual changes and growth within individuals' sociocultural backgrounds. Such teachers believe learning and development are culturally grounded and oriented; therefore, these are expressed in terms of multidirectional human actions in living rather than as predictable human developmental phenomena. Individuals' developmental growth and learning characteristics can be appropriately understood only within one's own cultural contexts.

Teachers' appropriate practices start with recognizing individual differences, simultaneously questioning the preexisting notion of "good" practice. Many "good" practices do not always work for all diverse learners. Teachers begin to have self-doubts: whether a "good" practice is culturally congruent with all diverse learners' learning styles; whether a "good" practice will positively affect everyone's learning and development. Attempts to individually base appropriate practices always remind the teachers to be willing to change and recreate their old belief in "good" practice including their own belief-system of learning and teaching, classroom management, assessment methods, communication styles, individual orientation, and so on. Teachers search for *many best ways* to support diverse individual learners' unique developmental changes and growth.

Therefore, teachers in an appropriate practice should always be in the habit of asking a situational question like: "What happens in the classroom, in this activity, in this lesson?" or "What happens in this practice? Can it be appropriate to John and/or Susan? Why? Why not? How about to Eunjoo? to Mark? to Kaya? Can this practice still be appropriate for these children and their families? Why? Why not? For such teachers, critical self-monitoring of the curriculum is on-going and inherent. Teachers' sense-making of what to teach and how to teach curriculum for appropriate practice is not single or scope-and-sequence oriented. Instead, it is more likely a lived curriculum--a teachable moment oriented curriculum, an emergent curriculum, as well as a negotiable curriculum--based on diverse learners' individual voices, needs, interests, and curiosities. Teachers are no longer ultimate power holders in any decision making. They become *active listeners* and *active learners* for themselves before they make any decision for appropriate practice in response to all culturally diverse learners' needs, as well as their parents' needs. Diverse voices from learners and their parents are the main agents in teachers' appropriate practice. Teachers, parents, and learners all share their power in the process of making decisions for appropriate practices. In appropriate practice, senses of shared power become pervasive among the members in classrooms.

Developmentally Appropriate Practice

Since 1987 in the field of early childhood education, there has been a guide known as Developmentally Appropriate Practice (DAP); it was originally suggested by the National Association for the Education of Young Children (NAEYC) (Bredekamp, 1987; Bredekamp & Copple, 1997).

The original DAP provided an important philosophical framework and set of related pedagogical guidelines in early childhood education, emphasizing age appropriateness and individual appropriateness (Bredekamp, 1987). Age appropriateness is important in that teachers need to be aware of children's predictable stages of growth in all developmental areas: physical, emotional, social, and cognitive. For individual appropriateness, teachers need to know and appreciate each child's uniqueness and individuality and to provide activities and materials that are personally interesting and challenging to that child. As a major mode for meeting the individual child's needs, child-initiated, child-directed, teacher-supported play is an essential component of developmentally appropriate practice.

However, educators and researchers have expressed their concerns regarding DAP as a "good" practice. They have critically examined DAP guidelines and questioned: whether DAP would provide developmentally and culturally congruent "good" practice for all diverse young children as individuals; whether it would guide teachers to create the optimal conditions for all diverse individual children; whether it would help teachers to realize the existence of human diversity and multiple perspectives on human change and growth in learning; whether it would support teachers into improving their curriculum so that it would be more sensitive to diverse learners' multiple voices and their perspectives. The guidelines seemed more culturally relevant to children and families from Euro-American cultural backgrounds than other ethnic backgrounds. Educators mentioned that DAP did not support an equal, fair, and culturally congruent teaching and learning experience, which meant critical thinking and practice was missing within the DAP for early childhood education.

In that mode of thinking, early childhood educators have identified the need for critical pedagogy when promoting education that is truly multicultural within the framework of Developmentally Appropriate Practice (Bowman, 1992, 1994; Bredekamp & Rosegrant, 1992; Delpit, 1988, 1995; Derman-Sparks, 1992; Hyun, 1996; Jipson, 1991; Mallory & New, 1994; Spodek & Brown, 1993; Swadener & Miller-March, 1993). The main criticism of the first edition of DAP was that it lacked multicultural sensitivity, that is, DAP did not fully promote *culturally appropriate* practice for *all* children. Therefore, there was a need for the DAP framework to represent Developmentally *and Culturally* Appropriate Practice (DCAP) (Hyun, 1995, 1996; Hyun & Dana, in press; Hyun & Marshall, 1996, 1997).

In response to the needs of culturally appropriate practice within the original DAP framework, NAEYC has revised and published a new edition of DAP guidelines (Bredekamp & Copple, 1997). The new guidelines highlight a body of knowledge regarding the social and cultural contexts in which children live and learn, along with the previously described two areas of age and individual appropriateness:

> ...the position statement defines developmentally appropriate practice as the outcome of a process of teacher decisionmaking that draws on at least three critical, interrelated bodies of knowledge (Bredekamp & Copple, 1997, p.vii):...
> 1. *What is known about child development and learning*--knowledge of age related human characteristics that permit general predictions within an age range about what activities, materials, interactions, or experiences will be safe, healthy, interesting, achievable, and also challenging to children;
> 2. *What is known about the strengths, interests, and needs of each individual child in the group* to be able to adapt for and be responsive to inevitable individual variation; and
> 3. *Knowledge of the social and cultural contexts in which children live* to ensure that learning experiences are meaningful, relevant, and respectful for the participating children and their families.(p.36)

DAP is described in this NAEYC definition as the outcome of a process of teacher decision making based on teachers' three areas of knowledge--age appropriateness, individual appropriateness, and children's social and cultural contexts. DAP is based on what is presently known and understood about children's growth and learning (Bredekamp & Copple, 1997; Bredekamp & Rosegrant, 1992; Gestwicki, 1995).

The definition and the foundation of DAP present critical limits in itself. Most presently existing bodies of knowledge regarding child/human growth and learning include almost no information about diverse ethnic cultures. Within the teacher education programs, it has been seldomly acknowledged that the dynamics of human growth and development are deeply affected either by group ethnic cultures or contemporary multiethnic family cultures. Furthermore, the new revised DAP guidelines do not specifically describe how to transform teachers' knowledge of DAP into experiences that are individually meaningful as well as culturally relevant to diverse young learners. The question, "What is the process of becoming DAP practitioners who can embrace culturally appropriate practice in their teaching to create culturally congruent interactions with all young learners?" has not been fully answered in the guidelines.

Teachers are required to be knowledgeable of individual children's social and cultural contexts that affect their developmental growth and learning. DAP should itself be a process that is always ready to change, to respond appropriately to the individual child's sociocultural family backgrounds when they are different from the teachers' own. DAP guidelines should require the teachers to become multiple perspective-takers in their process of decision making. How can teacher preparation programs prepare early childhood teachers to become developmentally and culturally appropriate practitioners for their teaching outcome of DAP for all individual children? What is developmentally and culturally appropriate practice? How do we infuse this process-oriented DCAP into teachers' everyday actions?

Developmentally and Culturally Appropriate Practice

Developmentally and Culturally Appropriate Practice (DCAP) is culturally congruent critical pedagogy that serves as a fundamental framework for early childhood education that is for all individuals. Critical pedagogy refers to classroom teaching that proceeds from a consideration of students' everyday lives and experiences (Giroux & Simon, 1989). It begins with several fundamental questions which can be raised by reflective teachers, such as: (a) What relationships do my students see between the activity or the work we do in class and the lives they live outside of our classroom? (b) Is it possible to incorporate aspects of students' lived culture into the work of schooling without simply confirming what they already know? (C)Can this incorporation be practiced without devaluing the objects and relationships important to students? and (d) Can this practice succeed without ignoring particular groups of students as "other" within a "dominant" culture? As evidenced through such questions, the notion of critical pedagogy is fundamental to education that is multicultural because "critical pedagogy is based on the experiences and viewpoints of students rather than on an imposed culture" (Nieto, 1992, p. 221).

Although pedagogical strategies for education that is multicultural continue to be discussed in various terms (see Table 1), they share one essential aspect: consideration of the learner's individual cultural background as shaped by his/her everyday experience at home or in the community. It is this importance of students' *home culture* that connects critical pedagogy to education that is multicultural. Successful early childhood education relies more on consistency between home and school cultures than on formal education at any other level. Thus, maintaining cultural congruency between young learners' home and school experience becomes the core of early childhood critical pedagogy for DCAP.

Developmentally and culturally appropriate practice is pertinent not only to ethnic groups but also to all young children who are experiencing new cultures as they grow, and as their family structure, cycle, and environment change. Table 2 presents the ways in which DCAP is derived from the notions of multicultural education, culturally congruent critical pedagogy, and anti-bias education. DCAP becomes an extension of DAP when combining the goals of multicultural education and anti-bias education with culturally congruent critical pedagogy. Teachers who adapt this particular framework into their own practice need to be aware of four major components as background knowledge for DCAP: Developmentally Appropriate Practice (DAP) (Bredekamp, 1987; Bredekamp & Copple, 1997), goals of multicultural education and appropriate messages for young children (York, 1991); Anti-Bias Curriculum (Derman-Sparks, 1989), and culturally congruent critical pedagogy (Hollins, King, & Hayman, 1994; Ladson-Billings, 1992; Nieto, 1992).

Table 1. Characteristics of Multicultural Pedagogical Strategies

Pedagogical Strategies	Characteristics
Cultural Congruence (Source: Mohatt & Erickson, 1981)	Implies one-to-one correspondence between what happens in school and what happens in the home; seeks consistency between children's home-school experience.
Cultural Appropriateness (Source : Au, 1993)	Requires being culturally proper or correct based on students' cultural background and experience; seeks optimal learning environment.
Cultural Responsiveness (Source: Erickson, Mohatt, 1982; Villeges, 1991)	Suggests that how people go about learning may differ across cultures; uses learner's culture as foundation of learning and teaching interaction.
Cultural Compatibility (Source: Jordon, 1985; Vogt, Jordon, & Tharp, 1987; Tharp, 1989)	Requires educational practices that match children's cultures in ways that ensures improvements in learning, including basic skills.
Mitigating Cultural Discontinuity (Source: Macias, 1987)	Considers that students of all cultures experience their first interruption of home-school-community nurturance and enculturation in school.
Cultural Relevance (Source: Ladson-Billings, 1992)	Serves to empower students to critically examine educational content and processes in light of creating a truly democratic and multicultural society; uses students' cultures to help them create meaning and understanding.

Table 2.   Basic Components of DCAP

Developmentally Appropriate Practice (DAP)

    Age Appropriateness

    Individual Appropriateness

    Social Cultural Appropriateness

    Play-oriented/Child-Initiated/Child-Directed Plan and Learning

Goals for Education That Is Multicultural and Appropriate Messages for Young Children

    Goals: Restructuring Schools for Equal Opportunity

- To help individuals reach their full potential so that they are in control

Function Cross-Culturally

- Knowledge
- Perception
- Attitudes
- Skills
- Patterns of behavior

Transform Curriculum for Knowledge Construction

- To help students become more aware of themselves as individuals and of their culture and/or cultures
- To help individuals develop an understanding of and appreciation for the cultures of others
- To encourage individuals to support and interact within many different cultural groups

Appropriate Messages for Young Children:

    Everyone is different from others: It is all right to be different.

    Differences are good and have value.

    Everyone deserves to choose how they want to live.

Table 2 (continued)

Everyone deserves the same opportunities regardless of gender, race, age, class, religion, physical conditions, sexual preference, family background, home culture and life, learning style, or communication style.

Anti-Bias Education

Goals:
- To change inequality and sources of stereotypes;
- To enable every child to construct a knowledgeable and confident self-identity;
- To develop a safe, empathic, just, and diverse interactive learning environment;
- To develop the knowledge and skills needed to stand up for oneself in the face of injustice.

Contents:

- People can change the social structures that perpetuate injustice;
- If the structure changes, people's attitudes will change;
- Students can be taught to take action against inequalities present in the classroom, school, and society regarding race, ethnicity, gender, language, religion, sex, physical and mental ableness, and class;
- Children need to be encouraged to do decision making, to act on their own choices, and be given opportunities to work cooperatively;
- Children can be taught skills of problem solving and critical thinking;
- Children need to be provided with experiences in taking social action.

Table 2 (continued)

Critical Pedagogy

Main Characteristics:

- Allows different students' voices to be heard and legitimated and takes the problems and needs of students as its beginning point;
- Accepts and uses students' experiences, culture, and language as learning resources;
- Respects and values different perspectives;
- Includes decision-making and social-action skills;

Culturally Congruent Critical Pedagogy:

Implies one-to-one correspondence between what happens in the home and the school; seeks consistency between children's home-school experiences.

Culturally Congruent Critical Pedagogy for Early Childhood Education:

- Allows and opens children to express and show the importance of their own family culture and identity;
- Employs children's personal experience, family culture, and diverse language expressions as important sources of learning and teaching;
- Respects differences in perceiving and understanding;
- Plans on the basis of the children's diverse ways of decision-making style and their social action skills.

As Table 2 presents, the goals of education that is multicultural support five possible messages for early childhood education that hold true to York's notion of affirming culture in early childhood programs. The goals of anti-bias education relate to five possible contents for early childhood education suggested by Derman-Sparkes and the A.B.C. Task Force. These goals, when combined to share teachers' work, are manifested through culturally congruent critical pedagogy that builds upon each young child's ethnicity, cultural background, and daily life experiences from home.

Based on this background knowledge, the teachers' dialectical thinking comes into play in their reflection, that is, by critically inquiring whether every child in the classroom has received an equal and culturally congruent teaching and learning experience for their developmental changes and growth. The teacher strives to learn about and understand each child's unique family influence which directly affects the child's development, learning, and problem solving skills. This dialectic leads the teacher to reflect on how she or he can use the child's unique background as a powerful instructional tool for all children in the classroom. This kind of fundamental reflective thinking used with the teacher's actual everyday practice would be called developmentally and culturally appropriate practice. Such reflection helps to ensure that the teachers consider multiple and diverse viewpoints as well as long-term social and moral consequences of their decisions. Teaching in this fashion will more likely result in education that is truly multicultural--that is for all children.

How can teacher preparation programs prepare early childhood teachers to become process-oriented DCAP practitioners for their DAP teaching outcomes? We need multiple approaches for DCAP early childhood teacher preparation (Hyun, 1996). The following chapters describe the multiple approaches that need to be readdressed, reintroduced, or restructured within preexisting early childhood teacher education programs for DCAP.

Chapter Two

Culture and Development in Children's Play

Children's play has been recognized as the major agent in young children's development and learning. Play also serves as an enculturative mechanism (Schwartzman, 1978). Through play children learn societal roles, norms, and values. Despite the limited and narrowed focus of the literature on children's play, several researchers and educators have recently proposed that children's play differs across cultures and socioeconomic status (Roopnarine & Johnson, 1994). As a fundamental concept for developmentally and culturally appropriate practice, we need to understand the dynamics of cultural influence and child development on children's play, particularly in the contexts of family ethnic culture. In this chapter I discuss the inseparable and culturally grounded relation between children's development and their play.

Culture Shapes Sense Making of the Phenomena

The eyes of looking at and interpreting children's play is different from culture to culture. Individuals with a strong influence from Euro-American cultural heritages look at, interpret, explore social phenomena on an individual basis. Especially when a person is raised by a Euro-American nuclear family, individualism is more apparent than when a person is raised by an extended or multigenerational family. The Euro-American ethnic perspective usually perceives that a family is composed of a few individuals.

In this context, individual independence, self-reliance, self-help, and autonomy are respected and encouraged (Becerra, 1988; Devore & London, 1993; Kain, 1993; Kitano, 1988; Locke, 1992; McAdoo, 1993; Min, 1988; Mindel, Habenstein, & Wright, 1988; Sanchez-Ayendez, 1988; Slonim, 1991; Staples, 1988; Stewart & Bennett, 1991; Szapocznik & Hernandez, 1988; Tran, 1988; Wilkinson, 1993; Williams, 1970; Wong, 1988). This individually oriented cultural mind-set shapes the researchers', practitioners', and parents' approach, understanding, and description of child's play phenomena within that paradigm. It also leads them to see interaction with the child based on that culturally shaped mode. For example, they are looking at whether the child can be in control of the play object, whether the individual child realizes that there are other individual(s), whether he or she is able to interact with them, how much same-age peer interaction occurs; or whether the individual child is able to negotiate with other individual(s) in a group play (Howes, 1980; Parten, 1933).

Psychologist Mildred Parten (1933) recorded the changing nature-- "development"--of young children's play from age two to age five. Parten's categories of children's social play have been frequently used since then. We still view her categories of child's play as a meaningful framework within which to examine the increasing social maturity of the child (Hughes, 1995). Her theory was based on the following developmental stages: (1) Solitary play. It is the lowest level of social play. The child plays alone and independently even if surrounded by other children. It is mentioned as typical of two-year-olds play; (2) Parallel play. The child plays independently at the same activity, at the same time, and in the same place. The child is aware of the presence of peers but each child plays separately; (3) Associate play. It is described as a common among three- and especially four-year-olds' play. The child is still focused on a separate activity but there is a considerable amount of sharing, lending, taking turns, and attending to the activities of one's peers; and (4) Cooperative play. It is described as a high level of play that represents the child's social and cognitive maturity.

The children can organize their play and/or activity cooperatively with a common goal and be able to differentiate and assign roles.

Influenced by Parten's theory, Howes (1980) and Howes, Unger, and Seidner (1989) present a similar developmental theory of child's social play: (1) Parallel play. Children engage in similar activities but do not pay any attention to one another; (2) Mutual regard. The child has an awareness of others but shows no verbalization or other social behaviors. The child only engages in a social act in similar or identical activities by making eye contact; (3) Simple social exchange. The child engages in similar activities along with other social behaviors such as talking, smiling, offering toys to peers; (4) Complementary play. The child shares common fantasy themes or engages in joint activities with a common goal, but makes no effort to integrate his/her own activities with another's; and (5) Reciprocal complementary play. The child begins to show a differentiation of complementary roles. One child is the leader in an activity, and one is follower (Johnson, Christie, & Yawkey, 1987; Hughes, 1995).

Following Parten's, Howes' and others' work, practitioners, educators, and parents who are from families with a strong influence of Euro-American culture tend to stress the cognitive benefits of child's play or the acquisition of individual independent social skills through play. They show thoughtful appreciation for child's play as a chief aspect of young children's everyday cognitive and social experiences that are individually oriented, independently based, or toy- or object-oriented (Johnson, Christie, & Yawkey, 1987).

Families with a strong African-American, Asian-American, or Hispanic-American background tend to be somewhat more group-oriented in their understanding of social phenomena compared to families from Euro-American cultures. There is a high tendency to have extended or multigenerational family structures. The individual is recognized as a member of the family group. They perceive family as composed of group members rather than individuals (Becerra, 1988; Devore & London, 1993; Kain, 1993; Kitano, 1988; Locke, 1992; McAdoo, 1993; Min, 1988;

Mindel, Habenstein, & Wright, 1988; Sanchez-Ayendez, 1988; Slonim, 1991; Staples, 1988; Stewart & Bennett, 1991; Szapocznik & Hernandez, 1988; Tran, 1988; Wilkinson, 1993; Williams, 1970; Wong, 1988). Within these cultural contexts family interdependence and family reliance are highly encouraged and expected. Thus, researchers from these cultural contexts focus on: whether the child receives frequent multi-age family interactions; within the family interaction, whether the child is emotionally happy and enjoys the play; whether the child is psychologically safe and relies on the family members in various forms of play. Based on this cultural frame of observing child's play, researchers report that during infancy and toddlerhood and even up to preschool children receive frequent child/parent, child/adult, multi-age child/child or child/children play opportunities within one's own family culture. The very young child is often in the middle of attending multi-age family-member play interactions, various forms of physical play with parents or multi-age family members. There is much eye contact, offering and receiving of toys, sharing, lending, turn-taking, and even organized cooperative play, which is all categorized by the Euro-American perspective as a high level of child's play and occurs in preschool years or older (Roopnarine, Hossain, Gill, & Brophy, 1994; New, 1994). Non-European researchers, teachers, and parents are somewhat more people-oriented, socioemotional, and multi-interactional rather than, individual-, sociocognitive-oriented.

Researchers and teachers with a strong Euro-American perspective tend to make sense of child's play and development based on how or what the child can do sociocognitively for oneself as an individual in the social context. With Asian-, African-, or Hispanic-American perspective the focus is on how the child can socioemotionally interact with family members and others as a group member. Therefore, these culturally different perspectives create a somewhat different line of understanding in child's play and their development. Even further, they value child's play and the developmental phenomena in culturally different ways.

We all have a culturally shaped frame of mind set. This culturally grounded phenomenon tends to lead people to believe that their ways of looking at things are universally acceptable, which may not be true. Thus, we all can become culturally blind.

Contemporary Cross-Cultural Perspectives on Children's Play

How we interpret child's play and development differs from culture to culture. Even defining child's play and a child's other activities differ depending on one's culture. For example, many families with Asian ethnic cultural influences tend to see play and academic activity separately. In contrast, from an Italian perspective, as in the Reggio Emilia schools in Italy, there is little distinction between play and child's other activities, and rather a strong emphasis on social-interaction in child's play (New, 1994). Many U.S. educators and researchers with Euro-American perspectives strongly believe that child-initiated play and other experiences are already related to the child's development of later academic experiences.

There is a cultural tendency of many families with Asian backgrounds to perceive child's play as a subject in itself rather than as a means for supporting academic experiences when the child becomes a kindergartner. Children tend to spend a great deal of their time in activities known as academically oriented experiences in their daily schedules (Pan, 1994; Takeuchi, 1994). These phenomena are highly valued and encouraged by the ethnic culture. In Spring of 1997, I did phenomenological interviews as well as field observations with Korean parents in Seoul, Korea and with Korean-American families in the New England area. Not surprisingly, these parents tend to strongly believe that academic activities are more highly valued than play, but within an academic activity the parents believe that children can enjoy it as a kind of play;

Academic activities are more important than play. Even if they are

> doing an academic work, they are still in a kind of play because they
> make it as a playful or fun study (interview with a Korean-American
> mother, Durham, NH, March 1997).

Even though their three-year-old child is engaged in an academically oriented activity--scribbling Korean and English alphabets, counting and scribbling numbers--once the child seems to be enjoying him/herself, parents join the activity with their child as a family activity. Many parents see it as a "Kongboo [study or academic activity]" that is fun and they highly encourage this kind of behavior as a "good" play. This kind of phenomenon can be easily observed in many families from Asian-American ethnic backgrounds throughout the United States.

As a cross-cultural phenomenon in child's play, children in contemporary industrialized social cultural contexts tend to spend a great deal of their play time in viewing television and performing often sedentary, individually oriented indoor activities (e.g., computer games, Nintendo), more so today than ever before (Takeuchi, 1994). These socioeconomical changes influence the children's traditional divergent play forms and affect whole aspects of children's developmental characteristics, particularly their socioemotional cognitive development and physical development. At the same time, each family creates somewhat new or different family values and practices in their child's play and is concerned with how to enhance or discourage play that would affect the child's development. These areas of study need to be as explicitly explored as other cross-cultural perspectives on play.

Many of these cross-cultural studies and theory developments were based on middle class populations using well-nourished children in controlled early childhood education settings. All children were assumed to be well-nourished not only physically but also spiritually and emotionally (Bloch & Adler, 1994). I am not sure whether these assumptions would be helpful in studying children from diverse socioeconomic contexts. Many children who are in poverty, homeless, and at risk may not follow the same developmental play stages as Parten's or well-nourished middle-class children. Their play-- its conditions, style, themes, and materials--is extremely diverse. How much do we know about these phenomena? Some early childhood monocultural teachers who are working with these culturally diverse children have a hard time in helping them. The teacher may even perceive that these children do not know how to play. She believes that one of her responsibilities is teaching the children how to play (see Ayers, 1989, Darlene's case). We need to investigate historically and socioeconomically underprivileged children's social and cultural conditions and their forms of play. Early childhood preservice and in-service practitioners need a fundamental framework that would guide them to see and understand diverse child's play. This area of study has not been explored.

The increasing number of multiethnic marriages and same-sex marriages, with children, has also created new and unexplored ethnic family cultures that affect child's play and development. If we are willing to accept the notion that culture shapes human growth and learning, we urgently need a contemporary cross cultural framework of understanding child's developmental changes and play that includes these emerging cultures. It would guide us more fairly and cross-culturally to understand child development and learning. It would also allow early childhood practitioners to interact with children in culturally relevant and congruent modes.

Limits on the Preexisting Notion of Child's Play

We have recognized the values of play, including play-oriented learning and experience, that are culturally contextualized. However, as I have noted, knowledge about child's play and approaches to understand child's play (Howes, 1980; Howes, Unger, & Sieder, 1989; Parten, 1933) have been mainly based on single-ethnic perspective which is variously called as Western middle-class, European,or Euro-American perspective. Roopnarine and Johnson (1994) point out that Euro-American mainstream ideas about play and early childhood education have not thoroughly considered certain cultural imperatives.

For more than six decades in the fields of social developmental psychology and early childhood education, researchers have been referencing Parten's or Howes' theory whenever they attempt to explore, understand, and assess young children's sociocognitive development through play, mostly within a single-age or same-age group setting. However, their conclusions are no longer accepted without question (Hughes, 1995). According to Parten, cooperative play begins to occur during the preschool years. Are all toddlers really unable to play cooperatively? It has been reported that children as young as eighteen months can sometimes cooperate in play with other peers, as when they play peek-a-boo or take turns by running after each other (Brenner & Mueller, 1982; Howes & Matheson, 1992).

In some family cultures, playful social exchange occurs as an inherent family interaction with their young child. A family with extended family members or a multigenerational family frequently has multi-age interactions. Within this sociocultural context, cooperative social interaction and social exchanges have been pervasive in the family culture. Becoming a cooperative player within a multigenerational and multi-age family environment and developing that kind of sociocognitive schema may be an inevitable developmental phenomenon. In this cultural context, the young child may first explore more about others than about self. Mentally visualizing play with others, observing others' intercommunicative expressions, being aware of the existence of family members or others in a play context are common phenomena that this young child has been receiving ever since birth. Thus, physically visualizing and cognitively realizing others during the early periods of childhood may be more apparent than the realizing of self as a single organism in such a child's developmental changes. Even though many European child development researchers have developed the theory that knowledge of self comes prior to knowledge of other, in this ethnic cultural context, knowledge of other may occur prior to knowledge of self. Realization of self may be a developmental phase that requires some degree of reflection of self with culturally shaped cognitive function because of the sociocultural influences. If we follow Parten's theory we may continuously underestimate or misunderstand the diverse young child's developmental abilities and potentials. More critically, we may be using some limited or culturally blind hypotheses to interpret the child's developmental changes and play behaviors.

On the other hand, if the child is from a nuclear family, particularly with a strong Euro-American cultural background emphasizing individualism, self-reliance, individual problem-solving, self-help, and autonomy, then interaction tends to be more object-oriented than multigenerational/multi-age people-oriented. Children have numerous opportunities to manipulate objects--functional and fully finished commercial toys for example--and discover properties and relationships. In Euro-American cultural contexts, the child may have a great deal of experience exploring objects and the relations between self and objects. Mentally visualizing play with toys and other objects and observing physical relations and the consequences may be phenomena that the child is cognitively facing. Thus, realizing and using one's autonomy may occur before the child is able to interact with peers or others of multi-ages. Parten's theory may be a culturally congruent framework to use in the study of child's play in Euro-American cultural contexts.

In addition, Parten's developmental framework has led researchers, educators, and parents to see solitary play by an older child as evidence of social immaturity. Yet, if we consider contemporary industrialized social culture, we realize there are various forms of child's play that are purely designed for solitary play. Are we still considering the seven- or eight-year-old child who daily plays computer games alone as socially immature? If we still follow the traditional approach to child's play, the framework is not only culture blind but historically out of date. Exploring and creating new understandings of child's play, deconstructing the old conventional orientation of child's play, and developing multiethnically and contemporarily relevant frames of reference for understanding child's play are urgent tasks for early childhood practitioners and families.

As an implication of this debate, early childhood teacher educators can give several exploratory assignment to the students. For example:

- Graduate level students: Conduct an ethnographic study of a contemporary multiethnic family's childrearing practices and their play interactions which affect the young child's developmental changes, growth, and learning.

- Undergraduate level students: Conduct formal or informal observations and interviews with historically and socioeconomically underprivileged families. Write a reflective and observational report on the experience and share it within a cooperative small group discussion.

A Story from the Field

Play is biologically based and is kept alive as an evolutionary contribution to human development and changes (Roopnarine & Johnson, 1994; Schwartzman, 1978). No matter how you define play, it is a dominant activity of children's daily life in all cultures. Children's play always portrays and reflects their own social values and family ethnic practices. Children play out personally meaningful experiences through their physical environment in their own way, while at the same time the sociocultural environment shapes children's play in its unique way (Erickson, 1963; Vygotsky, 1977). Play is an expression of a particular culture, including the child's own ethnic family culture; play is an important context or vehicle for cultural learning and transmission, as well as an indicator of child developmental changes and a reflection of their experiences (Schwartzman,

1978, 1983).

Children's ethnic family culture always interweaves directly in their play and peer interactions. Culture is the contextual factor that influences all forms of adult-child, child-child, and child-children play. The story that follows shows how a family's ethnic culture influences a teacher's thinking and action and children's play behavior. It is a story from an early childhood teacher's first-year experience. I met the teacher at a local private day care in Las Vegas, Nevada in 1988. The teacher's story is about a child name Eunjoo[1]:

Eunjoo is a Korean-American four-year-old girl. Every morning when the child comes into the classroom with her mother or her father, she and her parents bow to the teacher. Even though the teacher is not close by, they look for the teacher and once they have an eye contact with the teacher they all bow together to the teacher.

The first time they did that I thought, something must be wrong on my classroom floor. So I was a little panicked and rushed near them to check the floor but nothing was wrong on my floor. Later that day, I found a very interesting behavior of Eunjoo's. Several children were in the block area playing. Eunjoo just joined in the area. At the beginning she simply looked around, looking at others play and their block constructions. In the meanwhile she gradually moved one block to another from the shelves and began to build her own construction. At the moment I found out, I think I guessed that she was searching for a curve shape. So I found one and gave it to her. When she received the block, she was bending over her upper body looking at the block and the floor again. I was a little panicked again and thinking what's wrong on my floor. Right that moment,

I looked at Eunjoo's face. She was smiling at me and saying something in Korean with another bending-over behavior. Finally, right that moment I realized that she was bowing as her expression of thanks. I guess bowing is a socially very important behavior in their culture. After I figured it out, I was no longer panicked about my classroom floor whenever she and her parents bowed. Remember, this was my first week of my first job right after I finished college. I was nervous about everything. I guess, it was one week later,… in the morning after Eunjoo's father dropped her off and left the classroom, four boys in the class surrounded her and were following her and kept bowing at her. At first I didn't pay much attention. A couple minutes later Eunjoo came to me and tried to say something in English which I was not able to understan, what she was trying to say, but by looking at her sad face I could tell the boys made her unhappy and uncomfortable. I talked with them not to follow her anymore. Later, it was almost the end of free play time, I heard a loud crying at the housekeeping area. Eunjoo was crying. The four boys were laughing at her. One boy told me that they delivered mail to her in her house play. "When she received the mail, she bowed again so we laughed. Then she started crying." Oh poor Eunjoo! I had to help her. I really cared about her emotions right that moment. But I felt that I had no idea how to communicate it with her. She and I, we were so helpless. But we did have a very serious class group discussion talking about Eunjoo and her family's bowing practice being the same as when we say "thank you." I don't know how I actually led the discussion, but since then there have been no more happenings like that. Once in a while I saw other children bowing to each other with

Eunjoo. She had a big happy smile. I guess I survived, and
so did Eunjoo.

Without some knowledge and understanding of each other's family ethnic
cultural backgrounds, we can easily and unconsciously face a culture
conflict. It creates an early childhood classroom culture that is somewhat
unfair to all of the members of the classroom.

Critical Issues to Examine

I attempt to challenge early childhood practitioners to think and
analyze Eunjoo's case from different perspectives in order for us to be able
to expand our DAP to DCAP.

Was the teacher fair to herself when she interpreted the family's
bowing practice as a way of greeting or "thank you"? Was she able to make
sense of their behavior in a culturally congruent way not only to herself but
also to the family? At first she was only able to make sense of this bowing
behavior in her own culturally congruent way in the context of object-based
sociocognitive analysis, and affected by her nervousness as a new teacher.
Was she also able to reflect upon her own behavior from the parents'
perspective? In other words, did the teacher put herself into the family's
shoes to make sense of this situation properly and fairly? And what could she
do creatively to expand and enhance the culturally different children's
pretend/dramatic/role play so that it becomes individually and culturally
appropriate, fluent, and flexible? The teacher's first-person or single-ethnic
perspective-taking led her to be culturally congruent only to her own
experience. It created a limited, culturally blind, ethnocentric understanding
of both the child's play and the teacher-parent interaction.

Were the boys fair to themselves when they made fun of Eunjoo's
bowing behavior? How much and in what ways were they creative and
flexible about their cooperative role play? With a limited knowledge and

understanding of their own taken-for-granted cultural practices and their new peer's different sociocultural behavior which was also culturally limited, their creative peer interaction and cooperative play were problematic. Can these preschoolers become knowledgeable and analytical about their own and others' cultures using their metacognitive thinking? (In this case realizing that Eunjoo's bowing is the same as when others say "thank you.")

Was Eunjoo able to understand fairly why the boys made fun of her in the middle of play? Did Eunjoo know the fact that her teacher and peers in the classroom were not familiar with the bowing practice, but instead used verbal expressions such as "thank you" or "good morning"? Can Eunjoo process these cultural differences cognitively? How does she deal with the two cultures' mismatch and her resulting inner conflict regarding the bowing practice? At home bowing is highly valued, respected, and encouraged social behavior that affects Eunjoo's positive self-esteem, family-esteem, and self-identity; in the classroom, however, it is misinterpreted, disrespected, or ignored. How can the teacher and the parents help the young child to become an empowered bicultural and bilingual individual in that context?

Were Eunjoo's parents fair to themselves when the teacher looked at the classroom floor instead of responding (culturally) properly to their respectful bowing? Did Eunjoo's parents know that the teacher was not familiar with their ethnic family cultural practice? The parent and the child were also not likely to realize that the children in the classroom and the teacher would benefit in learning about some of their family ethnic cultural practices that are different from the teacher's and the other children's in the classroom.

The point here is that we all see, interpret, understand, and make sense of diverse social interactions based on a limited knowledge of self and each other. Thus, we are unfair to ourselves and limited in our lives which leads us to be first-person perspective-takers or single-ethnic perspective takers; one can only be culturally congruent to oneself.

There is a critical danger here especially to individuals in the education profession. The basic responsibility of education practitioners is to provide an equal and fair learning environment to all learners. In order for teachers to be able to create and maintain an equal and fair classroom culture for all, so that teachers' practice is not only equal and fair but also culturally congruent to all, the teacher should be a process-based practitioner who uses his/her own multiple and multiethnic perspective-taking.[2] Is this possible? If it is, how? Is there a clear guide in that regard in NAEYC's product-oriented DAP framework?

What would be both a developmentally and a culturally appropriate approach to solve this limit, and prevent this kind of cultural conflict in children's play and early childhood teachers' practice in the classroom? The key is the teacher. I suggest the following questions for early childhood teachers' process of decision making in their DAP work so that their practices actually become DCAP--that is, individually oriented and culturally congruent to all:

- What do I see? What do I hear?
- How do I interpret the situation (or the thing)?
- How can I be sure that my understanding of the child's behavior is culturally fair and appropriate to him/her?
- What leads me to think, interpret, and interact in that way (or mode) for the child? What are my cultural references on that matter?
- What leads the child (the parent, the children) to think, interpret, and behave in that way/mode? What are their cultural references on that matter?
- Is this a fair understanding for all of us about the conflict? Do all of us have enough knowledge of oneself and each other to understand the situation and solve the problem and conflicts that would allow us to create and maintain a culturally congruent and fair classroom cultures for all?
- How should we go about gathering and expanding our knowledge of oneself and others in this context to solve the conflict?
- How should we share the new necessary knowledge of this context and

use it properly to solve the conflict and create a fair classroom
culture for all?
- In what ways can I promote the children's play using the new
  knowledge so that all children become flexible and fluent in infusing all
  different cultural practices, while remaining free to enjoy their own
  cultural congruency within their creative play context.

Children's play is a universal phenomenon in human growth and
change that is culturally grounded and oriented, and it is a core of early
childhood education. How can early childhood practitioners incorporate this
important notion into their everyday DAP, so that their DAP becomes a
process-oriented DCAP for all culturally diverse individual children?
Examining one's own family ethnic culture and perspective is the most
fundamentally needed action with which we all need to start. Chapter 3
discusses this matter in more depth.

Chapter Three

An Autobiographical Approach Toward Developing Multiple and Multiethnic Perspective-Taking Abilities

In process-oriented teacher preparation for developmentally and culturally appropriate practice, developing one's own multiple/multiethnic perspective-taking ability is the main key. An autobiographical self-awareness approach, discussed in the first part of this chapter, is suggested for the initial approach to develop multiple/multiethnic perspective-taking. A later part of the chapter discusses development of multiple/multiethnic perspective-taking ability for teachers' DCAP.

An Autobiographical Self-Examination Approach to Diversity

Most multicultural educators and researchers agree that to function cross-culturally and to ensure an education that values diversity and multiple/multiethnic perspectives, prospective teachers must be helped to reflect on and examine their own cultural identity and values (Baker, 1994; Banks, 1994a, 1994b; Kincheloe, 1993; Nieto, 1992; Sleeter & Grant, 1994). Without awareness and acceptance of our own cultural values, we risk "cultural myopia," a failure to perceive the cultural differences between ourselves and those in other groups (Kumabe, Nishida, & Hepworth, 1985; McAdoo, 1993; Stewart & Bennett, 1991). An autobiographical self-examination of their own culture and values will help prospective teachers develop cross-cultural sensitivity necessary to make education that is multicultural--for all.

Prospective teachers should be helped to know, care, and act in ways that will foster learning and development in democratic classrooms. Through an autobiographical approach knowing more about oneself and others would occur naturally. Carefully planned and supported autobiographical reflection will help prospective teachers recognize their own and each other's individual cultural differences and how these differences are critically related to young children's learning and development. Self-examination serves as an important tool to develop one's own espoused platforms. Here, prospective teachers autobiographically reflect upon their own and other cultures. Doing so enables them to realize and value the significance of their own individual differences in an effort to foster multicultural sensitivity. Suggested inquiries for the prospective teachers' autobiographical approach are in Table 3. A systematic flowchart of these inquiries is available in Hyun and Marshall (1996).

Using the suggested inquiries I explored how early childhood prospective teachers develop multiple/multiethnic perspective-taking abilities through an autobiographical self-examination of their own culture and others (Hyun, 1997). The participants[3] of this study consisted of 201 prospective teachers who were enrolled in four different levels of field-based early childhood/elementary education courses, during Fall 1993 through Spring 1996, at either the Pennsylvania State University, University Park Campus, or Clarion University of Pennsylvania. Most of the participants were female students, eight were male. All identified their ethnic cultural background as "White" or Euro-American, except one female student who identified herself as African-American.

In the first class of each course, I introduced and gave an Autobiographical Self-Examination for Diversity questionnaire containing Table 3 inquiries. The format has 25 self-inquiry-oriented questions regarding cultures of self and family.

Table 3.

Suggested Inquiries in Autobiographical Self-Examination for Diversity

---

Who am I?

> Where does my culture come from?
>
> What was the culture of my parents and my grandparents?
>
> With what culture group(s) do I identify?
>
> What are the characteristics of my culture?
>
> What is the cultural relevance of my name?

How is my culture important?

Do I share it with others? How? Why? Why not?

Did my cultural background help me learning and living in school?

In what ways? or Why not?

How did I decide to become a teacher? What cultural aspects were
involved in the process?

What do I understand to be the relationship between culture and
education?

What unique abilities, aspirations, expectations, and limitations do I have
that might influence my relations with culturally diverse young children?

In what ways does my culture help me to be an appropriate practitioner
with children from diverse cultural backgrounds?

Do I have some specific culture in mind that I can most comfortably work with?

What allows me to think in these ways?

Do I need additional multicultural knowledge?

What additional multicultural knowledge do I need for my future as an
early childhood education teacher?

What can I do to achieve my needs?

How can my teacher preparation program serve my needs?

How do those needs pertain to who I am?

The prospective teachers in the courses had a week's time to do a
personal reflective essay based on the questions. They were encouraged to
explore their own cultural backgrounds within their family culture and to
respond to as many questions as possible, but responding to all the questions
was not required. In the second week of each course, the participants

engaged in a 30-minute small group discussion and then a 30-minute large group discussion to share their experience of autobiographical self-examination of their own ethnicity and family culture. As participant observer during the last part of the discussion, I posed some inquiries such as:

> How well do I know my own culture?
> In what ways did/does my culture(s) help me to become a teacher who can provide an equal and congruent learning experience for all children?
> How well do I understand education that is truly multicultural to promote a culturally congruent and equal learning environment for all the children I will teach?

After the discussion, all the participants were required to reflect on the discussion and express their thoughts in their academic journal.

During the semester we often discuss field-based questions in conjunction with the autobiographical approach. For example:

> How well do I know about the classroom culture?
> How do I interpret the classroom culture?
> What led me to interpret the classroom culture and the children's behavior in that way? How confident am I about my view on the diverse children's behavior and their learning styles that would allow me to interact with them fairly and in a culturally congruent way?

At the end of each semester, in their last class, the prospective teachers were asked to produce a self-reflective evaluation statement and to present it in a small group. This last activity gave them a chance to synthesize from all courses during the semester their learning experiences related to the autobiographical self-examination of their own ethnicity.

Their personal documents, academic journal, interview transcripts, and my participant note-taking were the main data collection. In the data collection I looked for reflections on the participants' personal understanding of their own culture and others' as means for developing sensitivity for diversity.

Several themes emerged from the participants' reflections. First, many students felt and said that they didn't know about their own cultural background because they had never been pressed by others to think about their own family culture. At the beginning of the semester most of the students felt that they were neither interested in this autobiographical assignment, nor saw its necessity or importance as part of their teacher preparation:

> At first, I had no idea about this project. I have never thought that I have a family culture that has impacted on me and my thinking and behavior. I mean I never had a chance to think about my culture. No one stressed this kind of issue for me to think about (Kelly, class discussion field note, Fall 1993).

> I went into the discussion feeling that my heritage had nothing to do with culture because it was never important in my family (Beth, journal entry 2, Spring 1996).

> I was very reluctant, at first, when writing the self-awareness paper. I could not see how my family culture would affect my teaching or the students. I soon realized, with the help of my group members, that we all bring something of our lives into the classroom (Gene, journal entry 3, Spring 1996).

Once they had spent some time thinking about it and discussed their own family culture in a small group, they began to think about this activity differently:

> When I began writing the assignment of last week [class discussion] on culture, I really didn't find it interesting. However, the more I thought about it and more opinions I heard from other classmates, the more interested I became...I found it very interesting to get into small groups to discuss our assignment. It made it a lot easier to speak about my paper. I wasn't nervous and I felt very open about it. It was also

> nice to hear about the specifics of other people's family cultures (Hess, journal entry 2, Spring 1996).

Furthermore, once they had a group sharing there was widespread feeling that the activity was an eye-opening experience, bringing them to discover about the "self" and "who they are." The activity also allowed them to exercise first-person perspective-taking, which allowed them to see the personal benefit of the activity:

> I felt that the self-awareness assignment really opened my eyes to some ideas that I really never thought about before...From doing the assignment and through our discussion in class, I have learned that my culture is what I believe in, the kind of person I am, and the way I was brought up (Patty, journal entry 2, Spring 1996).

> It made me look at myself in a way I never had before. It made me realize that my culture had more of an impact on my life than I thought it did (Nian, journal entry 3, Spring 1996).

> Overall, I felt this paper to be a great experience for me. I probably would not have asked myself so in-depth questions about culture. I now realize that it is part of me and it is so essential for me to know where I stand (Sandy, journal entry 2, Spring 1996).

> The autobiographical self-awareness project proved to be very educational to me. Culture is not something that I often think about. This project allowed me to take a look at my past and future (Shelly, journal entry 3, Spring 1996).

Second, through activity many of the prospective teachers realize the inseparable relation between culture and the individual, and the individual uniqueness that results from one's own cultural influences:

> I feel it is extremely important for a person to know who they are and where they come from so that they can help others understand what makes the individuals and their cultures so special (Wendy, journal entry 3, Spring 1996).

> An awareness of the fact that we all have something unique about our backgrounds which causes us to act a certain way... After the class discussion, it only seems logical that a person can't separate him/herself from their upbringing and it will affect them in almost any job setting, decision making, or many other factors in life (Linsy, journal entry 3, Spring 1996).

The autobiography activity also allowed the prospective teachers to see individual uniqueness based on family culture that is beyond ethnic or group/race orientation and led them to connect culture to the issue of equal education:

> I think it is important for future teachers to realize that not every child comes from the same type of background. In fact, any two children will never be the same. Teachers need to be aware of this and adjust their teaching style and strategies accordingly. This way, hopefully, all children can benefit and have an equal chance in education. Too many times in the past, teachers have ignored the fact that family background plays an extremely large part in how a child learns. I think that teachers need to learn as much as they can about each child as an individual. The teacher needs to recognize that differences are good and if everyone was the same life would be very boring (Sue, journal entry 1, Spring 1996).

Third, this autobiographical self-assessment has helped these prospective teachers to realize the importance of one's own culture and others', and thus led them to develop a conceptual sense of second-person perspective-taking ability from points of view other than one's own. This development expressed their metacognitive ability to comprehend and assume that another person might have a different but equally reasonable and valid cultural perspective:

> The self-awareness activity did help me to reflect on my own background and how I think of others. The activity actually made me think about what I think of my own culture, which is something I never really thought about before. But in doing so, I realize that it is

> important to me for other people to understand my culture, and in turn
> that others would probably feel the same way (Sharon's journal entry
> 3, Spring 1994).

> I think that my culture is important and it is my job to make my
> students feel that their culture is important too (Rochell, journal entry
> 2, Fall 1994).

Fourth, the autobiographical self-awareness activity helped the prospective to teachers look critically at other teachers' pedagogical behavior with children from diverse backgrounds:

> I began to realize its relevance. I now understand that how we were
> raised has much to do with how we will present ourselves in the
> classroom (Lin, journal entry 2, Spring 1996).

> I think it is especially important for Caucasian teachers to be sensitive
> and open toward other cultures and to feel comfortable with the
> cultures of different children. I also think it is important for Caucasian
> teachers not to impose "their" cultures on children of other cultures,
> which is sometimes done without even realizing it. Sometimes
> Caucasian teachers who are in the "mainstream culture" (so they may
> think), think that since these children live surrounded by the
> (mainstream) cultures, it is acceptable to gear the children toward it.
> I personally think that this should be avoided at all costs, and I think
> I will be successful at avoiding this because I am aware of it through
> this activity (Sharon's journal entry 3, Fall 1993).

Throughout each semester, the autobiographical approach led prospective teachers to realize the need for creating diverse interaction and teaching styles in conjunction with their development of second-person, third-person, and multiple/multiethnic perspective-taking abilities, which are cognitive abilities to step out of one's own limited value judgments and assume the existence of multiple realities in human living and learning, and the willingness to incorporate these realities into the practice of culturally congruent teaching and learning:

The student population is very diverse (racially, linguistically and ethnically) and this diversity is reflected in the books, the food, the language, the holidays and the activities that are taught...During calender and song time, children ask to sing and count in several (I think it's seven) different languages; children that aren't native English speakers are talked to, as much as possible, in their native tongue...The four teachers at Home for Children take concrete steps toward learning about different cultures, especially trying to learn about the different cultures in the classroom. There are children from Holland, Saudi Arabia, Korea, England. Most of these children have an extremely hard time each morning when their mom/dad leaves...The problem is that it is rather hard to console a child without being able to verbally communicate with him/her. One of the ways that they are dealing with this problem is that the teachers are trying to learn key phrases in the child's native language. There are sheets posted all over the center with appropriate phrases like 'Mommy will be back later this afternoon,' or 'Do you have to go to the bathroom?' written in both languages (Ana's journal entry 5, February 1995).

I ask the kids, 'Is there another way you want to count? What language?' They have Spanish, Haitian, Arabic, Korean, Siamese, Japanese, and French... (Ana, mid-term interview during preservice student teaching, March 1995).

Lastly, as a result of the prospective teachers' autobiographical activity throughout the semester, many student teachers expressed the need to have some basic knowledge of multiethnic family cultures in the United States. Having some basic knowledge of family ethnicity would be helpful for the prospective teachers' DCAP pedagogical development in guiding them to create an equal and culturally congruent teachers' practice:

Sometimes it's so hard because I don't know a lot of their backgrounds...I know where they're coming from like, some are from India. But I don't know their family backgrounds...how they're taught at home...I want to have a good interaction with the parents... I want to see what they are doing at home...I asked the parents, 'What are you doing at home with the children?' What are [you] reading at home with the children...What do they like? What do they dislike? I asked [them] to tell me the different words in your [their] language [so] that I could communicate with the children because I don't know what to say to a child if they are doing something wrong in the class or in my lesson...If they don't understand English I'd like them to at least know certain words (Mindy, final interview during preservice student teaching, Spring 1995).

The biggest obstacles...if I had four children, two of which were American and two were English as a second language [38 out of 45 students in the school use English as a second language]...I want to learn more for myself how to prepare lessons just for the English as a Second Language [students] because some of them would just sit down and just like would look around. It just touches my heart because I want them to all be focusing on the lessons but it's hard to because if the child doesn't understand...sometimes it's so hard because I don't know a lot of their backgrounds. I know where they're coming from like some are from India, Japan, Korea, ...But meaning like their family backgrounds like how they are taught at home...what the children were doing at home and I want to know...It's just so important by knowing that a teacher is going to get a lesson across to her children...Like some lessons might but others...Like for instance one little boy he may be disturbed in the classroom for no reason but he may have a problem at home and he brings that to school...that's another thing I want to know about if a child has problems at home...That's another big factor of mine: dealing with a child if he's abused... (Mindy, final interview during preservice student teaching, Spring 1995).

We should just try to develop a general knowledge of a few cultures and then over time keep expanding that knowledge base. I felt that this was a very good point that Kevin brought up because there are so many cultures that we could never learn everything about all of them...We all hope that we will be aware of these cultural cues that children send us because sometimes we may not have a lot of knowledge about their culture, and our communication may be limited due to language barriers (Karen, journal entry 3, Spring 1995).

Throughout the semester, I constantly found myself examining the relationship between culture and being a classroom teacher...I realize that teachers must be somewhat educated on the many different cultures that will be present in his/her classroom so as to meet the needs of the variety of children in the class. Possessing this knowledge will help make the class, and everyone else related to the class, be able to understand each other and what they are all about (Elley, reflective self-evaluation statement, Spring 1996).

I wish I could have some ideas on how to deal with the family life of some of my future students (Sara, reflective self-evaluation statement, Spring 1996).

DCAP and cultural awareness...these can only successfully be done if I am aware of the student's culture (Claire, reflective self-evaluation statement, Spring 1996).

Doing this autobiographical self-examination toward multicultural sensitivity in conjunction with field-based, process-oriented teacher preparation courses has helped the prospective teachers to see and realize the reality of the United States learner population and the critical needs of equal education and culturally relevant practices in the teaching lives of early childhood teachers. Bringing this fundamentally important experience into early childhood teacher preparation depends greatly upon the teacher educators' commitment to and ongoing practices of autobiographical self-examination as well as a strong belief in its effectiveness.

This study has given some clear evidence that the autobiographical approach with field-based teacher preparation courses creates room for prospective teachers to experience and develop multiple and multiethnic perspective-taking in relation with their growing sense of critical pedagogy, particularly as it deals with the need to practice equal education and diverse teaching styles in order to provide congruent learning experiences for all young children from diverse backgrounds.

Multiple/multiethnic perspective-taking is, in short, an individual's cognitive capacity to construct his/her understanding of self, other, and social phenomena through first-, second-, and third-person perspective-taking. The ability to step out of one's own cultural paradigm and assume that the existence of multiple realities inevitably leads to divergence in all human endeavor is the ultimate form of multiple/multiethnic perspective-taking. Multiple/multiethnic perspectives represent diverse peoples' diverse understandings of living, problem solving, learning, and so on, as derived from not only their intra-ethnic phenomena (each family's ethnic and cultural formation that is unique to their own "group" ethnic cultures) but also their inter-ethnic relations (ethnic "group" culture that interacts with each individual family culture) as explained further in the next section.

Developing Multiple and Multiethnic Perspective-Taking Abilities[4]

What are the in-depth phenomena of teachers' multiple and multiethnic perspective-taking in relation to the development of critical pedagogy for early childhood education? How do we develop this way of thinking and acting?

Researchers and educators often argue that while students with diverse backgrounds have some unique ways of learning, they share many learning characteristics with other groups (Banks, 1994a, 1994b; Ramirez & Castaneda, 1974; Stodolsky & Lesser, 1967). This argument has led to the over-simplified labeling of students' learning styles, such as "field-dependent/independent" or "reflective/impulsive" (Ladson-Billings, 1992). To the extent that such labels cast the teacher as a passive facilitator, realizing interactive concerns between students' learning styles and teaching styles becomes problematic.

Traditional notions of learning and teaching styles must change (Marshall, 1994). Learning is affected not only by the learners' style, but by the ever changing interactive mix that includes the teacher's style, social and cultural contexts, and the curriculum in use. Even those with similar cultural backgrounds have somewhat different ways and levels of understanding

(Gardner, 1983). Teachers of young children should learn to explore multiple perspective-taking through field-based processes in order to better understand each child's learning styles and the child's potential of learning development. In doing so, the teacher develops a repertoire of diverse teaching styles for her/himself (Hyun & Marshall, 1997).

DCAP rests upon a culturally congruent teaching and learning environment; it is dynamic and responsive to teachers' observations of and interactions with the children they teach. DCAP encourages teachers' inquiry into children's developmental changes and learning styles, based on learners' unique individual/family cultural characteristics, so that they can translate their knowledge into appropriate pedagogical practices. DCAP also empowers teachers in their work with young children and contributes to their own creative teaching development. In this section, I discuss how to enhance people's perspective-taking from single to multiple perspective-taking so that teachers can find out about other learners' learning styles and develop their own divergent teaching styles.

Orientation

Teachers in the United States are primarily white and female, coming from middle-class backgrounds, and with limited exposure to racial/ethnic and economic diversity. Without a focus on developing a pedagogical sense of DCAP for early childhood education, teachers in preparation will remain inadequately prepared to respond appropriately to all diverse young children. Teacher educators must provide theory and experiences which enable prospective teachers to become multiple/multiethnic perspective-takers. Prospective teachers typically have a limited understanding of their own selves and their family ethnic backgrounds--limits which affect their learning, development, and ways of pedagogical thinking. Most students in higher education scarcely recognize that their pedagogical beliefs have been guided by single-ethnic perspective-taking (Hyun, 1995).

When development and learning are inseparable from the sociocultural context, new assumptions related to appropriate teacher preparation vividly emerge. In a diverse society, teachers must deal with multiple perspectives, value systems, and various forms of human development that are divergent, multidirectional, and positively impacted by family culture (Cannella & Reiff, 1994; Sizemore, 1979; Sleeter & Grant, 1994).

Without developing their own multiple/multiethnic perspective-taking abilities, teachers cannot create developmentally and culturally congruent and fair learning and teaching experiences for all other learners. Developing perspective-taking involves coordinating and integrating various psychological perspectives--specifically, first-, second-, and third-person perspectives. The ability to assume a second-person perspective allows people psychologically to step out of their egocentrism (first-person perspective-taking) or cultural myopia to comprehend that another person might have a different, although equally reasonable perspective. Teachers who have the ability to integrate the first(self)- and second-person perspectives can see themselves through the eyes of others and evaluate children's behavior through these eyes. Table 4 provides examples of these varied phases of teachers' inner dialogue perspective-taking:

Table 4.

Varied Phases of Teachers' Inner Dialogue in Perspective-Taking

Soonja doesn't know how to greet people properly. One is expected to say 'How are you?' or 'How do you do?' when you meet people. She must be a shy person or doesn't know this type of social interaction well. **(First-Person/Single-Ethnic Perspective-Taking)**

Instead she bows and/or simply says 'Hi' or 'Hello' and drops her eyes for a short moment. I notice that Soonja is greeting others in a different way

Table 4 (continued)

compared to my style of greeting, yet it seems to be socially appropriate and personally meaningful behavior to her...**(Second-Person/Bi-Ethnic Perspective-Taking)**

In some cases, Soonja uses 'How are you?' with a person who is personally closer to her than others who she simply knows. But even when she has a close relationship, if the person is older than her, it seems to me she does not use "How are you?" but rather 'Hello' or 'Hi.' Somehow, these distinctions seem to reflect appropriate social distinctions. Now that I think about it, many people use different style/ways of greetings in their social contacts while maintaining an appropriate degree of social interaction. I guess my style is just one of many greeting practices....**(Third-Person/Multiple/Multiethnic Perspective-Taking)**

As illustrated above, the third-person perspective permits a teacher to add another dimension to her social-cognitive abilities by allowing him or her to step out of the teacher's own cultural paradigm, which tends to be a collection of individually distinct elements. Cognition of one's own culture becomes less context specific as she or he generalizes across distinct, culturally diverse situations. In addition, this third-person perspective allows one to generalize across groups. Ethnic perspective-taking as socially constructive cognition can, therefore, lead to multicultural perspectives which require one to understand others within a context of inter-ethnic and intra-ethnic dynamics (Quintana, 1994).

Quintana's theory suggests that realizing the existence of multiple realities inevitably leads to divergence in all human endeavor. This divergence can be found in human development, cultural and educational values, and even in ways of learning and teaching. According to Quintana, a person with little bicultural experience may have limited development of his or her own ethnic perspective-taking ability. That is, for many children and adults, there may be a lag in their social perspective-taking development, depending on the extent of their experiences with, understanding of, and appreciation for their own and other ethnic groups. People limited to monocultural experiences may be significantly delayed in the development of ethnic perspective-taking ability, relative to their social-cognitive abilities. As Cannella and Reiff (1994) report, prospective teachers with largely monocultural experiences may be significantly limited in their multiethnic perspective-taking ability. This is unfortunate because it is a fundamental ability for the reflective teachers' use of developmentally and culturally appropriate practice (Hyun, 1995).

Developing multiple/multiethnic perspective-taking ability--for use in teachers' everyday pedagogical practices--ought to be standard practice in teacher education programs. Teachers in a diverse society require a high level of cognitive capacity that allows them to understand how to connect with all learners' unique capacity to make sense of the learners' learning. This cognitive social capacity can lead teachers to construct developmentally and culturally congruent pedagogy that creates an equal and fair learning environment for all individuals with diverse learner styles and capacities.

To develop this multiple/multiethnic perspective-taking ability, teacher educators must first examine and come to understand their own monocultural experiences through autobiographical self-examination of one's own culture, then expand to include bicultural/cross-cultural and multicultural experiences. This is particularly important for those with limited ethnic or cultural experiences. To be successful perspective takers in a diverse society, new teachers should develop their multiple/multiethnic perspective-taking ability during their initial teacher preparation experience.

To accomplish this, it may be helpful to consider a conceptual construction that points out the simple parallel dynamics between perspective-taking and ethnic perspective-taking ability within the phenomena of Interpersonal Negotiation Strategies[5] (Selman & Schultz, 1990). After the autobiographical self-examination of one's own culture activity, I suggest, it is time to introduce the conceptual understanding of these parallel dynamics to the students in any pedagogical course or in-service workshop.

Parallel Dynamics of Perspective-Taking and
Ethnic Perspective-Taking Ability

Table 5 introduces parallel dynamics between perspective-taking and ethnic perspective-taking. The stages are recursive given the nature of a person's inner dialogue; that is, a person may move back and forth between and among them, rather than following the stages in an invariant sequence from first to last. Individuals will constantly reconstruct diverse perspective-taking in light of their various social and cultural contacts. Consequently, self-awareness of one's own cultural paradigm (i.e., autobiographical self-examination toward diversity, Table 3) becomes the cornerstone to expanding one's own multiple/multiethnic perspective-taking.

Because each new social contact may bring a cultural conflict, most adolescents and adults start thinking in a first-person/single-ethnic perspective-taking manner. However, knowing that their interpretation of others may limit a genuine understanding of them, self-conscious, reflective persons consciously remain willing to expand their own perspective-taking to second-person, third-person, and multiple perspective-taking. Therefore, individuals' self-examination of their own cultural paradigm coupled with an ongoing, inner dialogue are key to bringing about this recursive dynamic and producing teachers who have multiple/multiethnic perspective-taking ability.

Table 5.

Parallel Dynamics of Perspective-Taking and Ethnic Perspective-Taking Within Interpersonal Negotiation Strategies

---

First-Person Perspective-Taking = **Single-Ethnic Perspective-Taking**

Egocentrism, ethnocentrism, and cultural myopia direct the person's thinking and behavior. Knowing about self and examining one's own cultural paradigm which has formed one's own thinking and behavior are limited. Expectations of others' sense making of living, learning, problem solving approaches, etc., are based on one's point of view, which is derived from one's own family background. Inappropriate or unfair value judgments regarding others may occur in the person's social interaction.

Second-Person Perspective-Taking = **Bi-Ethnic/Cross-Ethnic Perspective-Taking**

Ability to comprehend and assume that another person might have a different but equally reasonable perspective. Knowing about self and examining one's own cultural paradigm are active and on-going, simultaneously, in a one-to-one interaction. Expectations of others' sense making of living, learning, problem solving approaches, and so on, that are based on one's point of view are reconstructed and changed. Personal "inner negotiation" with the other person occurs frequently, leading one to develop cross-cultural competencies and to be willing to solve conflicts with others.

Third-Person Perspective-Taking = **Multiple/Multiethnic Perspective-Taking**

Ability to step out of one's own cultural paradigm and assume that the existence of multiple realities inevitability leads to divergence in all human endeavor. Expecting diverse and multiple ways of making sense of living or learning provides diverse problem solving approaches in any social context. Realizing that there were, are, and always will be multiple perspectives in a human society, and that these multiple perspectives have been derived from each individual's unique family ethnicity, this individual family ethnicity is valued and treated equally. This realization leads to a willingness to explore, learn about, and respect diverse perspectives from various family ethnic practices.

Pedagogical Thinking and Action with
Multiple/Multiethnic Perspective-Taking

In order for teachers to provide developmentally and culturally congruent learning experiences that serve all young children, teacher educators need to pay attention to the dynamics of perspective-taking in prospective teachers' thinking and action in conjunction with their various interpersonal negotiation strategies (Selman & Schultz, 1990). Table 6 presents examples of teachers' perspective-taking as it's implemented in their pedagogical reflective thinking and instructional action.

Table 6.

Phases of Teacher's Multiple/Multiethnic Perspective-Taking Ability and Interpersonal Negotiation Strategies Implemented Through Pedagogical Thinking and Action.

Phases of Perspective-Taking
First-person Perspective-Taking = Single-ethnic Perspective-Taking

Interpersonal Negotiation Strategy (INS): One-Way INS
Orientation: Use power-oriented negotiations including one-way commands and orders or conversely, simple and unchallenging accommodations (giving in) to the perceived needs and demands of the other person.
Thinking: Children should use only English because that is only language I, as their teacher, can understand.
Action: Akia!, you should be using English in the classroom. Than I will understand what you say.
Pedagogical Phenomenon: This type of interpersonal negotiation strategy may lead teachers to the habit of high levels of survival or task focus in their pedagogical practices. In this case we can easily observe teachers who are overly concerned with classroom management and control. A high frequency

Table 6 (Continued)

of teacher directive, one-way instruction and limits on learner oriented reflective practices become main elements of classroom culture. Teachers expect students to adjust to teaching styles rather than modify instruction to fit students' learning needs.

Phases of Perspective-Taking
Second-person Perspective-Taking = Bi-ethnic/Cross Ethnic Perspective-Taking

Interpersonal Negotiation Strategy (INS): Reciprocal INS

Orientation: Use psychologically based reciprocal exchanges that coordinate the perspectives of both self and other in the ability to reflect upon the negotiation from a second person perspective. It is understood that both self and other are planful and self-reflective, and that the thoughts, feelings, and actions of each influence those of the other. Strategies include psychological trades and exchanges, verbal persuasion or deference, convincing others, making deals, and other forms of self-interested cooperation.

Thinking: Maybe Akia feels somewhat uncomfortable using only English in the classroom. If I were Akia I would feel more comfortable using my own familiar language at first.

Action: Akia, when you want to talk about something, you may use the language that is most comfortable for you. It can be either your own family language or sometimes it can be English. Perhaps you could teach me some of your language so that I can know what you are thinking and feeling.

Pedagogical Phenomenon: Teachers examine means and goals by asking self-questions in order to make independent, individual decisions about pedagogical issues.

Phases of Perspective-Taking
Third-person Perspective-Taking = Multiple/Multiethnic Perspective-Taking

Interpersonal Negotiation Strategy (INS): Mutual INS

Orientation: Represents a consideration of the need for an integration of the

Table 6 (Continued)

interests of self and other so that the negotiation is viewed from a third-person perspective. These strategies involve compromise, dialogue, process analysis, and the development of a shared goal of mutual understanding. There is an understanding that concern for the relationship's continuity over time is a necessary consideration for the adequate and optimal solution of any immediate problem.

Thinking: Maybe other children want to know or learn about Akia's home language and her own unique ideas too. Maybe there are other languages the children know/use from their family culture which I have not noticed yet.
The children may also want to share those. By inviting the children to share their own family culture/practices the child him/herself will be able to create a congruent learning experience between home and school. It would also be beneficial to other children to expose diverse language expressions, divergent learning experience,s and various ways for problem solving.

Action: Ask the children in the classroom about what other languages we are using/can we use/or want to use. "Let's count the numbers in Akia's home language." Can we think about any other language we can use to count the numbers?" Encourage the children to learn about each other's language,
unique ideas to solve a problem, etc. And then let them share within the formal peer interactions or formal instructional learning events.

Pedagogical Phenomenon: Teachers are both process-and outcome-oriented. They examine classroom phenomena from multiple perspectives and recognize how the decisions they make influence the learning that occurs. Teachers look critically at the ethical bases of what happens in the classroom and determine how exact practices affect all learners.

Teachers who are mainly in the habit of first-person/single-ethnic perspective-taking often feel that some children are "especially" different than others based on group ethnicity, physical traits, on socioeconomic status, and naively hope that these different children will follow the teachers' instructions and "fit in" some day as others do. Since culturally diverse children are surrounded by mainstream or dominant culture, teachers usually believe that it is correct to move children toward the mainstream (i.e., the teacher's) learning expectations. This type of "power pedagogy" creates a hidden curriculum in which individuality goes unrecognized and an unfair learning environment is inherently accepted within the classroom culture. Within this classroom culture, the true meaning of an equal education thus becomes subconsciously muted.

However, once teachers elect to expand their instructional perspective-taking from first-person/single-ethnic perspective-taking to second-person/bi-ethnic perspective-taking, developmentally and culturally congruent learning and teaching can begin to take place for each individual child. Simultaneously, more equal power sharing tends to be present between the teacher and individual learners within the classroom culture. If teachers can learn to move in and out of first- and second-person perspective-taking, the traditional institutionalized power struggle between "minority" learners and teachers from the dominant culture may fade away eventually.

Ultimately, it is the teacher's ability to develop third- person/ multiple/multiethnic perspective-taking that will result in genuine developmentally and culturally appropriate practice within the classroom. Teachers who initiate and encourage multiple power sharing by inviting all learners' voices, ideas, and decision-making opportunities into the learning experience become members of multiple peer interactions instead of the sole power holder of students' learning. Within a DCAP-based classroom culture, learners are encouraged to create their own developmentally and culturally congruent learning experiences by incorporating their own languages, experiences, and knowledge through a pedagogy which respects the true meaning of education for all individuals. Genuine DCAP results in a classroom culture which reflects reciprocal, diverse, and fair power sharing through the expression of each individual learner's unique presence as facilitated through a learner-oriented, continuously negotiable, and socially constructed curriculum.

Implications for DCAP Teacher Education Courses

Diverse implications follow from an autobiographical approach in developing multiple and multiethnic perspective-taking. One sequential approach is as follows:

Phase 1: Autobiographical self-examination of one's own culture and group sharing and discussion (Use Table 3 or Hyun & Marshall's [1996])

Phase 2: Introduce examples of varied phases of teachers' inner dialogue in perspective-taking (use Table 4 and Table 5).

Ask the students to explore personal reflective inner dialogue using any daily life incident in which there may be a certain degree of cultural conflict.

Ask the students whether they can identify their inner dialogue in three different perspective-takings as in Table 4. Have students share their experiences in a small group discussion.

Phase 3: Introduce Table 6; Phases of Teacher's Multiple/Multiethnic Perspective-Taking and Interpersonal Negotiation Strategies Implemented Through Pedagogical Thinking and Action.

Ask the students to reflect on any classroom incident (pedagogical issue, disciplinary issue, management issue, teacher-child interaction, teacher-children interaction, child-child interaction, or child-children/peer interaction issues) that shows a certain degree of conflict.

Ask the students to identify/describe their style of problem solving or approach to the conflict.

Ask the students whether they can extend or change their problem-solving skills or way of approaching the conflict by considering Table 6.

Ask what alternative approaches they come up with after the in-depth exploration and why they think their alternative approaches might work to help create a positive and fair classroom culture and individual-based DCAP learning experience. Have them share their ideas in a small cooperative group.

Have the cooperative group members give some other ideas or suggestions to each other.

This approach can be implemented in a course which has a field-based component or on-site workshop for inservice practitioners. It will enhance the preservice and the inservice teachers' development of reflective teaching and ongoing self-evaluation. This experience would be particularly effective in a field-based workshop with a group of preservice and inservice teachers with diverse levels of experience.

In addition, this chapter should be helpful in any introductory education course that deals with human growth, change, and learning, particularly in dealing with social cognitive development. This fairly new theory of multiple/multiethnic perspective-taking ability is different from the theory of social perspective-taking (Selman, 1980) and Piaget's (1952) conventional theory of child's developmental perspective-taking. The theory of multiple/multiethnic perspective-taking is directly related to teachers' social-cognitive pedagogical behavior. Thus, it is hoped that the new theory will affect teachers' future professional practice in creating a pluralistic society.

Implications for the Field

Current trends in the United States teacher education are more multicultural and more field-based than ever before (National Council for Accreditation of Teacher Education, 1979; 1992; 1994, 1997). Within the mode of field-based multicultural teacher preparation, teachers' DCAP and multiple/multiethnic perspective-taking are inseparable. Implications of this theory focus particularly on infusing it into initial teacher preparation course work--particularly field-based courses, including preservice teaching and student teaching, as well as inservice programs. The parallel dynamics of social and ethnic perspective-taking (see Table 5), phases of teachers' multiple/multiethnic perspective-taking, and interpersonal negotiation strategies implemented through pedagogical thinking and action (see Table 6) can all be discussed easily and appropriately in field-based courses as an orientation for clinical experiences. As clinical guides, these frameworks can help teacher educators, prospective teachers, and inservice teachers explore and analyze their pedagogical practices based on certain phases of perspective-taking in relation to their current teaching experience. The frameworks will also challenge and expand their reflective practices and understandings about true multicultural teaching and developmentally appropriate practice in general.

Additionally, this theory brings together ideas about the human cognitive capacity of multiple/multiethnic perspective-taking and ideas about teaching. Clearly, empirical research pertaining to its efficacy with regard to pedagogy in general, and teacher education in particular, remains to be done. Particularly, we should investigate prospective teachers' processes of change and growth in incorporating multiple/multiethnic perspective-taking ability. Examples of teachers' pedagogical practices illustrating this ability and their reasons for using it need to be carefully constructed and shared.

As Fuller (1992) suggests, initial teacher preparation programs should require procedures which lead prospective teachers to better understand, be sensitive to, and appreciate self and diversity so that they can create equal and culturally congruent opportunities for each individual learner in their classrooms. All teachers, in part, base their practice upon what they believe about people, society, culture, and values. Yet for many of them (both novice and experienced teachers), these beliefs come deeply and subconsciously from their own first-person/single-ethnic perspective-taking. Egocentric and subjective perspective-taking prohibits teachers from providing developmentally and culturally congruent, fair teaching and learning experiences to all individuals. Thus, helping teachers to enhance their multiple/multiethnic perspective-taking ability is critically and fundamentally needed not only for early childhood teacher education but also for overall teacher education programs.

Teachers can and do make conscious, significant decisions about teaching from multiple perspectives when they employ not only their own, but second- and third-person multiple/multiethnic perspectives. Using various levels of theory-based cognitive potential in teacher education programs can help teachers develop this multiple/multiethnic perspective-taking ability. Prospective teachers should encounter opportunities to witness and experience these various levels of perspective-taking during their teacher preparation period. Examples of such practices include using field-based/reality-oriented case studies in courses (e.g., Shulman & Mesa-Bains, 1994) that emphasize mental more than written lesson planning for the prospective teacher's instructional multiple/multiethnic perspective-taking development (Hyun & Marshall, 1996). As teacher educators, our challenge is to find even more meaningful ways for this to happen.

This chapter has suggested a new area of study that combines cognitive psychology and teacher preparation. For two decades, NCATE guidelines have required new teachers to be prepared to practice "education that is multicultural." At the same time, many researchers and teacher educators have questioned whether this mission is fully possible. Perhaps the approach presented in this chapter can provide both research and practice directions that will bring us closer to accomplishing this mission.

Chapter Four

Ways of Studying Culture and Ethnicity

Being knowledgeable about family ethnic cultures that affect young children's development and learning enhances the teachers' multiple/multiethnic perspective-taking abilities in their DCAP. Many educators and researchers (Banks, 1994a, 1994b; Larke, Wiseman, & Bradley, 1990; Locke, 1992) recognize a critical need for greater knowledge of culture and ethnicity in multicultural education. Banks (1994b) mentions that, once teachers have gained knowledge about cultural and ethnic diversity themselves, looked at that knowledge from different ethnic and cultural perspectives, and taken action to make their own lives and communities more culturally sensitive and diverse, then these teacher will have the knowledge and skills that are critically needed to help transform the curriculum for equal and fair education. Larke, Wiseman, and Bradley (1990) also advise that "the more knowledgeable teachers are about the cultures of their students and the more positive interactions [there are] between teachers and students of different racial/ethnic groups, the less threatened and acceptable teachers and students become of each other's cultural differences" (72).

People limited to monocultural experiences may be significantly diminished in their multiethnic perspective-taking ability (Cannella & Reiff, 1994; Quintana, 1994). Prospective early childhood teachers are overwhelmingly white and mostly female, come from strong Euro-American middle-class backgrounds, and have limited exposure to racial/ethnic and economic diversity. Like most educators, they are inadequately prepared to respond appropriately to all diverse learners (Fuller, 1992; Goodlad, 1990; Ladson-Billings, 1992; Trent, 1991). Of all their concerns, preservice early childhood teachers feel least confident about how their work will coincide with the childrearing practices of culturally diverse families about whom they know very little (Hyun, 1995; Reiff & Cannella, 1990). These limited experiences virtually guarantee classroom culture shock (Cannella & Reiff, 1994)

Within our field, family ethnic diversity should be studied as a form of pedagogical knowledge. Those at work with young children need help to develop multiethnic perspective-taking abilities using the knowledge of family ethnicity. They can also be helped to recognize that cultural influences on learning and development become valuable pedagogical knowledge for them as they learn to adapt curriculum and instruction to the unique needs of young children from diverse cultural, ethnic, gender, and social groups. Early childhood teachers who work with diverse ethnic children and families will be far more effective if they have and incorporate accurate information about their students' unique family cultures and ethnic backgrounds within the learning environment (Hyun, 1995; McAdoo, 1993). This chapter discusses ways of studying and teaching culture and family ethnicity to enhance teachers' multiple/multiethnic perspective-taking.

The Need for Introducing Family Ethnicity in
Early Childhood Teacher Preparation for DCAP

The United States is moving toward a time when a majority of its citizens will be members of an ethnicity beyond social classes, racial groupings, regional differences, and even countries of origin. Ethnic identification has evolved so that it now transcends individual differences and has become family ethnicity, or the identification of entire families or clusters of individuals. Ethnicity is understood as family ethnicity. It is fundamental to individual identity. Family ethnicity involves unique family structures, customs, proverbs, and stories that are passed on for generations. It includes celebrations, traditional foods, religious ceremonies that are shared, and the stories of how the first family members came to this land, childrearing styles, child-parent/child-adults/child-child(ren) play styles, values and beliefs, ways of solving problems, and so on. Our family ethnicity is one of the most fundamental elements of our being (McAdoo, 1993; Mindel, Habenstein, & Wright, 1988).

Early childhood education has more and stronger demands in terms of school-home, school-family, and school-parent relationships than any other education level. According to Derman-Sparks (1992) and Ramsey (1987), early childhood education has a great need to examine the family values and beliefs that underlie childrearing practices and ways of being in the world.

Early childhood teacher preparation programs need to help prospective teachers to: (a) have a fairly clear knowledge of the values of the "dominant" culture (Locke, 1992) as well as to see that Euro-American or "White" American ethnicity is not universal and that even within the ethnic group there are great differences in each family ethnic culture; (b) see the values that each ethnic group practices that make them feel good about themselves and support healthy, positive self-identity and family-esteem; (c) reflect how to make their future classrooms more like the children's homes, where children have learned to be powerful and self-confident; and (d) learn how teachers can help children transfer their self-confidence into the classroom which is perceived as another new cultural setting by the young learners.

Characteristics of Family Ethnicity

In order to provide the pedagogical knowledge of family ethnicity for DCAP in early childhood education, I present in this section a general frame of reference for understanding culturally apparent characteristics of major ethnic groups in the United States (See Table 7). To deal with ethnic characteristics is a vast idea. Yet, early childhood practitioners should at least understand a few characteristics of family ethnicity which directly affect young children's developmental changes, learning, problem solving, and social adjustment. If a child is from a strong single ethnic background--for example, African-American, Euro-American, Asian-American, Native-American, or Hispanic-American--the child would feel more comfortable with the teacher who has at least some general knowledge of the particular cultural practices that directly affect the child's growth, learning styles, problem-solving styles, and communication styles.

A child cannot be understood in isolation from his/her family and environment (Slonim, 1991). These generalizations for understanding family ethnic characteristics need to be used within a cultural context. And they should be seen as value free, nonjudgmental guidelines for curriculum development for all young learners.

According to Slonim (1991), there are distinct cultural differences in each ethnic group, and the various cultures within an ethnic group are not homogeneous. Yet there are some similarities within an ethnic group for historical, philosophical, or geographical reasons. Based on these similarities, Slonim and other cross-cultural psychologists present a general frame of reference for understanding the major ethnic cultures in the United States. I strongly emphasize that generalized similarities are merely guidelines for understanding behavior within a cultural context.

The similarities among people from a strong Asian-American background are mainly philosophical, based on Confucianism and Buddhism. But there are also distinct cultural differences in heritage, life-style, language, and childrearing practices. Similarities of the various Hispanic-American cultures are from Iberian heritage, language, and influence of the Roman Catholic religion. "Traditional characteristics are rapidly diminishing or changing, especially as a result of migration. Many of these traditions exist today only among the people who are in poverty and have a limited formal education. Still, it is important to consider their origin and to be aware of their lingering influence" (Slonim, 1991. 164). The cultural heritage of blacks in the United States is identified as African American. Their family cultures have roots in their African heritage based on (1) the kinship group and tribal survival, and (2) marriage as a union of families, not just individuals. These kinship bonds provide the basis of political, social, and economic organization. These are a set of core values and behavior that remain distinctively characteristic of and understood by a majority of African-American families. However, there is no such entity as "the typical African-American family" anymore than there is a "typical White family," or "typical Asian family." Each family is unique and must be considered in terms of its own heritage and understood within a cultural context (Slonim, 1991).

In terms of the demographic changes in the 1990s and beyond the year 2000, African-American, Asian-American, Hispanic-American, and European-American are the major ethnic groups in the United States (McAdoo, 1993). These four groups' family ethnic characteristics are introduced here. These characteristics are generalizations about each ethnic group, and there are always great variations in each individual child and adult within each group and each family. It is important to acknowledge variations in family structure that can lead to variations in adaptation to social and economic circumstances despite culturally shared meanings and styles (Sanchez-Ayendez, 1988). There is much literature that describes general United States family ethnic group cultures. Table 7, Characteristics of Cross-Cultural Family Ethnicity, is based on the work of cross-cultural psychologists (Stewart & Bennett, 1991) and sociologists (Becerra, 1988; Devore & London, 1993; Kain, 1993; Kitano, 1988; Locke, 1992; McAdoo, 1993; Min, 1988; Mindel, Habenstein, & Wright, 1988; Sanchez-Ayendez, 1988; Slonim, 1991; Staples, 1988; Stewart & Bennett, 1991; Szapocznik & Hernandez, 1988; Tran, 1988; Wilkinson, 1993; Williams, 1970; Wong, 1988).

The kind of knowledge in Table 7 should be introduced with a explicit assumption and a careful awareness. For example a family with a strong ethnic cultural influence from Euro-American backgrounds (or African-American, Asian-American, or Hispanic-American) tend to have certain family cultural characteristics that seem to affect the child's developmental characteristics, learning styles, problem-solving styles, communication styles, and so on. But some families are not clearly representative of their own ethnic backgrounds; they may look more contemporary with combinations of other ethnic influences because of many factors, including their years of being in the contemporary United States culture, geographical location, occupations, same-sex marriage orientation, multiethnic marriage status, and so on.

This assumption and awareness should be discussed by the teacher educators before they introduce this general frame of reference to either prospective teachers or inservice practitioners. This will allow early childhood practitioners to be more responsible observers in making developmentally and culturally appropriate decisions in their teaching.

Table 7.
Characteristics of Cross-Cultural Family Ethnicity
(Table 7 continued to p.70)

Extended/Nuclear Family

Euro-American: Mostly nuclear family.

African-American: Extended family plays a vital role for most African Americans. Many children see parents, grandparents, uncle, aunts, and cousins as a part of everyday life.

Asian-American: Extended rather than nuclear family: Most often, an elderly parent lives in the same household as the adult children.

Hispanic-American : Most Hispanic families have an extended or multigenerational family.

Table 7 Continued

Role of Family Members

> **Euro-American:** Individually oriented. Most males and females tend toward a relationship of equals.
>
> **African-American:** Wife or women in family are highly independent. The male-female marital relationship has been characterized by more egalitarian roles and economic parity than "White" culture.
>
> **Asian-American:** Hierarchical family relations; parent expects absolute obedience from their children; husband expects the same from his wife.
>
> **Hispanic-American :** Male dominance has been prominent. The older family members of their extended family can take a role as the religious teachers, family historians, nurturers of small children, and transmitters and guardians of accumulated wisdom. Although husbands have been the traditional source of family authority, most of the decisions concerning childrearing are made by the mothers.

Expectations among Family Members

> **Euro-American:** Highly individualistic; self-reliance, individual problem-solving, and autonomy are emphasized.
>
> **African-American:** Females are encouraged to be independent rather than passive individuals because many of them may carry family and economic responsibilities alone. Taking on adult responsibilities is something many children from African-American backgrounds learn early.
>
> **Asian-American:** A great Confucian ethical influence exists: respect, obedience, and filial piety to parents and ancestors are highly emphasized along with observance of rank order, from children to parents, and from wife to husband. An individual is expected to be loyal to his or her family and obey and respect elders. Asian-American children show greater concern and devotion toward their elders than most children from other ethnic backgrounds.

Table 7 Continued

Hispanic-American : The family is a major support system. Key to the family system is the value of sharing and cooperation. To its members the family remains the strongest source of emotional strength, support, security and a sense of belonging. Rigid sex and age grading is observed whereby the older orders the younger, and the men the women. Family interdependence is conceptualized as positive.

Childrearing and Discipline

Euro-American: Interaction with children is object oriented. Children have numerous opportunities to manipulate objects and discover properties and relationships. Self-help is emphasized.

African-American: Children tend to be more feeling oriented, people oriented. Communication can be nonverbal. Children are expected to receive affection and comfort and learn to give it when it is needed by others.

Asian-American: The father maintains his authority and respect by means of a certain amount of emotional distance. Discipline is more strict than that which the typical American child receives. The child is expected to behave as an adult. Aggressive behavior on the part of the young and sibling rivalry are not tolerated and but rather all strongly discouraged. Many traditions and cultural values are strongly related to their history and their ancestors. Children learn socially approved patterns of behavior at a very early age and also what others think of them. Instead of individual guilt governing their behavior, the sense of face, or shame to themselves and to their family acts as a major form of social control.

Hispanic-American : Most Hispanic-Americans easily show two distinguishing aspects in their childrearing: (1) the reinforcement of sex-role distinctions through childrearing practices, (2) support and assistance through extended family. Childhood is a warm and nurturing period and children receive much attention and affection. Childrearing practices   reinforce dependence rather than independence.

Table 7 Continued

Kinship Relationship

Euro-American: In most cases individual relations are a little bit stronger than kinship relations compared to other ethnic groups.

African-American: Kinship system among Afro-Americans tends to be interdependent and multigenerational. In many cases maintenance of an extended network of kin is functional for modern urban African-American families.

Asian-American: Many Asian-Americans feel that relatives are a more important source of help than friends. They maintain active social interactions with their kin members.

Hispanic-American: Generally, close relationships with maternal and paternal grandparents are fundamental. Of special importance are the emotional ties with the mother's relatives. Maternal aunts often serve as brokers, providing a link as "second mothers" or mother substitutes.

Values and Beliefs

Euro-American: Doing and being active are highly valued. The human being is perceived as separate from and superior to nature.

African-American: Kinship, group loyalty, mutual support and compassion, and adaptability are highly valued. Family and church are esteemed as sources of strength, consistency, and identity.

Asian-American: Many values and beliefs come from the Confucian ethic, which puts more emphasis on the past than does American culture. Materialism is not so important as in American culture. Working hard, and being diligent and industrious are the important traits to survive and succeed in society.

Hispanic-American: Face-to-face relationships are very important. There is a great emphasis on the present. This emphasis more accurately reflects a relaxed concept of time in which people are considered more important than schedules and there is total absorption in the task at hand.

Interpersonal Characteristics

Euro-American: Emphasizes individualism and privacy. Informal and direct friendships are numerous but not as deep or permanent as in other ethnic

---

Table 7 Continued

groups. Social obligations are less important.

African-American: Highly sensitive to others' nonverbal cues. Greeting always include inquiries about people who are important to the person, in contrast to certain greetings which discuss the weather and rarely inquire about human life and conditions.

Asian-American: The public display of affection is considered in poor taste by many Asian Americans. Respecting each other is an important attitude in interpersonal relations. Interactions are more formal and structured than Euro-American culture. The social obligation network takes on an important role in interpersonal relations.

Hispanic-American: Interpersonal relations are strongly related to various ways of sharing, such as sharing foods. Generally sensitive to others' feelings and observant of rules of conduct such as respect for the status of others. People are respected for their knowledge of the history of the community, ethnic group, and for having more experience in life.

Education and Learning Characteristics

Euro-American: Prefer an object-oriented, analytical approach to learning. The main learning teaching approaches are functional and emphasize solving problems independently and accomplishing tasks.

African-American: Novelty and inferential reasoning have an important role in learning. Cooperative decision making in learning is emphasized. Providing human interaction in the learning process is important. Being socially well-educated is important to the eyes of the community.

Asian-American: See education as a formal process. Teachers are to be highly respected. Humility is an important virtue. Reading of factual information is seen as valuable study. Sometimes academic achievement takes over social or family obligation.

Hispanic-American: Looking, touching, and having peers react to each other create appropriate learning experiences. Education is conceived as a

---

Table 7 Continued

means of social mobility but not as an end in itself. Cooperation is valued more than competition in learning. Being socially well-educated is more important than being academically well-educated.

Identity

Euro-American: Self is identified with individual. Behavior is aimed at individual goals. Self-esteem is emphasized.

African-American: Family relations or family esteem is perceived as key in individual identity.

Asian-American: See the individual as part of the whole society in somewhat a selfless view. Family esteem is emphasized.

Hispanic-American: In many cases self is perceived in context of family and the relations. Family esteem is emphasized.

Attitudes

Euro-American: View people in fragments or react to them in terms of isolated parts or roles rather than as a total personality.

African-American: Traditional African beliefs strongly influence the perception of health as related to the degree of harmony or discord in one's body, mind, and spirit. Often sociocentric, feeling-oriented, people-oriented, and proficient at nonverbal communication.

Asian-American: A person who has a good listening behavior is valued as a person of a good attitude. You should be polite, quiet, patient, and humble to become a respectable person.

Hispanic-American: Maintaining personal loyalty to friends is important. Members of this group are sensitive to praise and criticism.

Problem solving

Euro-American: Prefer to reason inductively. Place a high value on self-reliance and autonomy. Encouraged to solve own problems and develop own opinions.

Table 7 Continued

> **African-American:** Cooperation is used as an valuable approach. Many of them use internal cues for problem solving.
> **Asian-American:** Dependence is not deplored because it strengthens relationships among family members and people in general.
> **Hispanic-American:** Dependence for problem solving is acceptable because group members believe that it strengthens relationships among family members and others.

Table 7 presents aspects of family ethnic characteristics that are related to diverse young children's backgrounds in learning, developmental changes, and social adjustment. When early childhood teacher preparation programs introduce these ethnic characteristics to prospective teachers, they need to use them extremely carefully so as not to make any assumptions about cultural characteristics in a way that would negatively influence a truly pluralistic society. It is particularly important for the prospective teachers to use this basic frame of knowledge the first time they try to understand the importance of child's play in the individual child's overall developmental changes and growth. Children's play is not only the core of young children's growth and learning but is also a reflection of their ethnic family culture and self-image. What are appropriate strategies for implementing this cultural knowledge so that it can be carefully transformed into early childhood teachers' pedagogical knowledge for play-based DCAP teaching?

Implementation of Cultural Knowledge in Teaching

According to Renwick (1974), once you have studied and learned about the fundamental characteristics of both your own culture and the culture of the person with whom you are now in conflict, your perceptions of the other person are more accurate than before. Because of your new knowledge and new perceptions, your attitudes may be open to the other person, and you may be more willing to understand the other's point of view and deal confidently with the conflict. Given your knowledge, perceptions, and attitudes, you may be able to use your new skill to explain your own position in a way that the other person can understand, and you may be able to analyze cultural differences without making any value judgment. By doing so you practice and develop new models of relating and communicating as one pattern of your behavior. Based on Renwick's notion of knowledge, perception, attitudes, skills, and patterns of behaviors, I introduce phases of instructional approach to study family ethnicity that incorporate and enhance the development of multiple/multiethnic perspective-taking abilities (see Table 8).

Table 8.

Phases of Instructional Approach in Implementing Culturally Congruent Learning (Table 8 continued to p.72)

Phase	Instructional Implementation
Knowledge	Examining autobiographical self-awareness for diversity (Chapter 3, Table 3), reading and learning about cross-cultural family ethnic characteristics (Chapter 4, Table 7)
Perception	Discussing personal images of others' backgrounds (Chapter 3, Table 4's example of three phases of inner dialogue as a model)
Attitudes	Sharing ideas to begin to open to others and being willing to deal with cultural conflicts in class

---

Table 8 Continued

Skills	Being able to explain why a particular child behaves/solves problems/interacts with others in a particular way by using the various perspective-taking tools (Chapter 3, Tables 4 & 5) and putting him/herself into the child's situation
Patterns of behaviors	Trying to practice and develop a culturally congruent learning and communicating experience for diverse young learners (Chapter 3, Table 6)

The knowledge phase should be incorporated with Chapter 3's autobiographical self-examination approach, and reading and discussing literature on ethnic family characteristics in the United States. Exemplary resources are;

Kumbe, K. T., Nishida, C., & Hepworth, D. H. (1985). *Bridging ethnocultural diversity in social work and health.* Honolulu: University of Hawaii, School of Social Work.

Locke, D. C. (1992). *Increasing multicultural understanding: A comprehensive model.* Newbury Park, CA: SAGE.

McAdoo H. P. (Ed.). (1993). *Family ethnicity: Strength in diversity.* Newbury Park, CA: SAGE.

Mindel, C. H., Habenstein, R.W., & Wright, R. (1988). (Eds.) *Ethnic families in America: Patterns and variations.(3rd edition).* Englewood Cliffs, New Jersey: Prentice-Hall.

Slonim, E. (1991). *Children, culture, and ethnicity: Evaluating and understanding the impact.* New York: Garland.

Stewart, E., & Bennett, M. (1991). *American cultural patterns: A cross-cultural perspective.* Yarmouth, ME: Intercultural.

In this phase of instruction, you can ask the prospective teachers to visit several ethnically diverse families with young children (from infant to age eight) in their communities. The teachers need to observe the family childrearing and disciplinary practices and play interactions of parent/child, family member/child, or child/sibling(s) to find out anything new or different from what they thought before about family culture and child play. In this process the prospective teachers need to collect data to add to their own expanding knowledge of ethnic family cultures and how they affect young children's developmental changes and learning as reflected in child's play.

The perception phase needs some real case study approaches such as I described in the sample inner dialogue in Chapter 3, Table 4. Prospective teachers need to reflect on any personal episode from field observation or field experiences from which they can develop an autobiographical inner dialogue in either written or verbal form. Let them share their dialogues within a small group as the beginning of an exploration of attitude phase. In *the attitude phase*, group discussion members can bring diverse perspectives to help solve a cross-cultural misunderstanding or conflict which took place during the field observation. The group sharing can also produce an eye-opening experience in understanding the existence of not only inter-ethnic but also intra-ethnic differences between observer and family or within the family. This experience will help the early childhood prospective teachers to picture the need for diverse teaching approaches, different physical arrangements and conditions, and diverse interaction styles that should be culturally congruent between home and school for individual child.

The skill phase, you can ask the prospective teachers to review Chapter 3, Table 5 (Parallel Dynamics of Perspective-Taking Ability and Ethnic Perspective-Taking Ability Within Interpersonal Negotiation Strategies), using the teachers' field-based cases. This process will allow them to articulate their own conflict or limited understanding of an individual child's developmental characteristics in various perspectives to benefit the child's school life as well as the teachers' professional growth. This process will enable teachers to explain why some children behave or play in such ways and solve problems differently with unique styles and skills of communication.

For *the pattern of behaviors phase*, the prospective teachers need to make a connection to their DCAP pedagogical practice that would create an equal, fair, and culturally congruent learning and teaching environment. I suggest using Chapter 3, Table 6; Phases of Implementing Teachers' Multiple/multiethnic Perspective-taking and Interpersonal Negotiation Strategies. Prospective teachers are advised to think and create an early childhood class environment that will support individual child's home language, his/her family's unique childrearing practices and play interactions. In this phase, I strongly suggest that teacher educators bring many exemplary DCAP practices from other experienced teachers into the class discussion. Various formats for reviewing experienced teachers' practices can be used, such as video tape, pictures, slides, role play, guest speakers' presentation, workshop, on-site visits, or on-site observation and discussion.

Phases of knowledge, perception, and attitudes lead to the prospective teacher's development of first-, second-, and third-person perspective-taking abilities. These can be implemented within the conventional teacher preparation class experiences. If the teacher preparation courses are all field-based, the phases of skills and patterns of behavior, which are multiple/multiethnic perspective-taking oriented, can be implemented more easily than in conventional-classroom-oriented course work experiences because of the prospective teachers' actual classroom contacts with the diverse learners. I strongly suggest you study ethnic family cultures and the instructional approach outlined above in any child development course and in courses on child's play and family relations. I would especially recommend that you use this approach at the beginning of the course before prospective teachers are exposed to "conventional" or "universal" approaches to learn about child development, child's play, and parent involvement. Their fundamental orientation for early childhood education should not be racially blind, ethnically blind, or culturally blind. Rather, their practice should be individual family based and teacher reflective.

Chapter Five

Field Experience and
Inquiry-Oriented Reflective Supervision for DCAP[6]

In order to be successful in early childhood teacher preparation for DCAP, we also need to provide inquiry-oriented reflective supervision for the prospective teachers' formal field experiences (Hyun & Marshall, 1996). Such supervision focuses on helping teachers become reflective practitioners who routinely take reflection-in-action, and who are both process and outcome oriented. Such teachers examine classroom phenomena from multiple perspectives and recognize how the decisions they make influence the learning that occurs. Teachers look critically at the ethical bases of what happens in the classroom and determine how to extend practices that will affect all learners. This chapter focuses on DCAP's integration within student teaching field experience and its supervision.

Many teacher preparation programs currently work to promote the preparation of reflective teachers (Bowman, 1989; Lubeck, 1996; Schon, 1983; Valli & Taylor, 1988; Waxman, 1988), most importantly because the wide range of classrooms and the diversity of students and cultures in today's schools require teachers to be divergent thinkers who are highly flexible and sensitive. Reflective teaching can, therefore, promote education that is multicultural for all (Grant & Zeichner, 1984).

Colton and Sparks-Langer (1992) extend the importance of the teacher as reflective practitioner by highlighting teachers' expanding decision-making roles. Today's teachers are being encouraged to make more of the major decisions affecting their own schools--schools with an increasing population of diverse learners. To respond successfully to these diversified students, we need to prepare teachers who can make their own judgments based on thoughtful and reflective inquiry, analysis, and appropriate assessment. In short, tomorrow's early childhood teachers and practitioners must be prepared to be thoughtful, reflective, self-directed decision makers capable of providing developmentally and culturally appropriate practice to achieve education that is truly multicultural: for all young children.

Once prospective teachers have a good foundation in DCAP (resulting from process-based early childhood teacher preparation coursework), they must have a chance to employ this knowledge in a practical sense. Thus, planning and implementing culturally congruent critical pedagogy serves as the final anchor of early childhood teacher education for developmentally and culturally appropriate practice.

The Reality in U.S. Education

Nissani (1990) predicted that by the end of the 1990s many United States school districts will serve a majority of students from ethnic, linguistic, and racial minority families. According to McAdoo (1993) and Rix (1990), more than one out of four current United States residents are nonwhite or of Hispanic ancestry. If present trends in immigration and birthrates continue until the end of the twentieth century, Trent (1991) predicts that within United States schools, the Asian-American presence will increase by 22%, the Hispanic-American presence by 21%, the African-American presence by 12%, and Americans of European descent by only 2%. Many students of color will more likely continue to be poor and live within single-parent, mostly-female headed households with frequent absence of a positive male figure. Thornburg, Hoffman, and Remeika (1991) note that many children are at risk from not only physical but spiritual poverty; that is, drugs, low-income working or/and single parents, child abuse, institutionalized racism, and so on. The present situation requires that teachers be well aware of the multicultural reality of the regular classroom.

At the same time, the nation's teaching force is changing inversely in relation to these shifting demographics (Ladson-Billings, 1994). Teachers are overwhelmingly white and mostly female; they come from middle-class backgrounds with limited exposure to racial, cultural, linguistic, ethnic, and economic diversity. As such, teachers are inadequately prepared to respond appropriately to changing school populations (Goodlad, 1990; Ladson-Billings, 1994; Trent, 1991). As Fuller (1992) recommends, we need teacher preparation programs that enable preservice teachers to better understand and appreciate diversity, and preservice field experiences and student teaching sites that provide prospective teachers with exposure to children from diverse populations.

Since 1979 the National Council for Accreditation of Teacher Education (NCATE) standards have contained a multicultural education component. The newly revised NCATE standards (1992, 1994, 1997) and NAEYC guidelines for preparation of early childhood professionals address multicultural education perspectives explicitly. Standards that pertain to clinical and field-based experiences require that:

> Field-based and clinical experiences are systematically selected to provide opportunities for education students to observe, plan, and practice in a variety of settings appropriate to the professional roles for which they are being prepared... Education students participate in field-based and/or clinical experiences with culturally diverse and exceptional populations (NCATE 1992, 51).

> Fields experiences---programs prepare early childhood professionals who...work effectively over time with children of diverse ages (infants, toddlers, pre-schoolers, or primary school age), with diverse abilities, reflecting culturally and linguistically diverse family systems (NCATE 1994, 244; NCATE 1997, 280).

Although the standards exist, and although accredited schools presumably "meet" such standards, simply seeing that early childhood education preservice students have such placements does not necessarily mean that the students become more appreciative of diversity. That kind of assurance remains the responsibility of teacher educators, student teaching supervisors, and the programs they represent.

Teacher preparation programs need to practically facilitate prospective teachers' reflection upon the meanings of demographic changes in the classroom. To bring developmentally and culturally appropriate practice into early childhood education we must help prospective teachers learn how to reflect upon their teaching with diverse learners and, through reflection, how to become classroom decision makers who will transform the challenges inherent in social, cultural, economic, racial, and ethnic diversity into opportunities and possibilities for all young learners.

The Needs of Inquiry-Oriented Reflective Supervision for DCAP

Reflective Teacher Preparation

According to van Manen (1991), reflection is a fundamental aspect of educational theory and practice, and in that sense it becomes synonymous with thinking about teachers' pedagogical practices (Lasley, 1992). Table 9 briefly presents types of reflection, teachers' stages of pedagogical practice, and how reflection can occur within these stages.

Novice teachers are typically at the first stage of pedagogical practice and reflectivity (Fuller & Bowen, 1975; Lasley, 1992; van Manen, 1977). However, teaching is much more complicated than it appears when depicted as a stage or developmentally oriented hierarchical phenomenon. Nonetheless, when understood heuristically, the organization of ideas found in Table 9 can permit prospective teachers to begin appreciating the need to develop habits of reflective thinking and practice. In time, and with experience and support, teachers will need to achieve the ability to be critically reflective in order to fully succeed at developmentally and culturally appropriate practice.

The value of an organized display of ideas like that of Table 9 rests in its ability to help us make sense of the nature and purposes of pedagogical reflection. Despite the developmental aspects of such reflective processes, reflective teachers will move back and forth within such a framework as situations present new challenges to them (Kagan, 1989). For example, if an experienced teacher wants to move away from teacher directive toward more learner directive instruction she/he is likely to experience initial concerns about technically oriented aspects resulting from her efforts to change than philosophical or ethical aspects. This illustrates the recursive nature of reflective pedagogical practice as veteran teachers revisit earlier points in their development while attempting to cope with new and different situations. Thus, a stage or developmentally oriented depiction of reflection relative to pedagogical practice need not be understood as a static, final representation: each stage or developmental level is different though not universally "better" than another, depending upon circumstances, and each one is important at various points in time.

Efforts to facilitate the prospective teachers' desire and ability to reflectively practice in developmentally and culturally appropriate ways require further consideration of the elements and natural dynamics of reflection. Table 10 represents the nature of reflective practice (Killion & Todnem, 1991; Schon, 1983) and its elements (Sparks-Langer & Colton, 1991). From Table 10 we see that the nature of reflective practice represents a mental process related to teachers' actions. The goal of reflective practice in teacher education toward developmentally and culturally appropriate practice is to help prospective teachers become comfortable with reflection-in-action during their preservice practicum. Within most teacher preparation programs, the supervised, clinical context of student teaching serves as the best place to develop this practice.

Table 9.

Types of Reflection Relative to Pedagogical Practice

Types of reflection	Stages of pedagogical practice	Reflection within stages of practice
Technical reflection: Teachers consider the effective application of skills and knowledge about teaching.	*Stage I: Survival focus:* Teachers are often concerned with classroom management and control.	*Instrumental focus:* Teachers reflect on technical issues such as identifying and dealing with specific problems.
Practical reflection: Teachers examine means and goals by asking self-questions in order to make independent, individual decisions about pedagogical issues.	*Stage II: Task focus:* Teachers expect students to adjust to teaching styles rather than modifing instruction to fit students' learning needs.	*Conceptual focus:* Teachers try to understand philosophical and theoretical bases for classroom practice and to foster consistency between espoused theory and philosophy.
Critical reflection: Teachers consider the moral and ethical issues of social compassion and justice.	*Stage III: Impact focus:* Teachers are both process and outcome oriented. They examine classroom phenomena from multiple perspectives and recognize how the decisions they make influence the learning that occurs.	*Dialectical focus:* Teachers look critically at the ethical bases of what happens in the classroom and determine how extant practices affect all learners.
Sources: van Manen, 1977; Zeichner & Liston, 1987	Sources: Berliner, 1986; Fuller & Bowen, 1975	Sources: van Manen, 1977; Glickman, 1990; Lasley, 1992

Table 10.

The Nature and Elements of Reflective Practice

The nature of reflective practice	Elements of reflection
Reflection-in-action: refers to reflection in the midst of practice.	*Cognitive element:* concerned with knowledge that teachers need in order to make good decisions in and about classroom situations.
Reflection-on-action: essentially reactive with reflection-in-action.	*Narrative element:* provides a much richer understanding of what takes place in classrooms and in teachers' construction of reality.
Reflection-for-action: the desired outcome of reflection on & in-action.	*Critical element*: concerned with the moral and ethical aspects of social compassion and justice.

Reflective phenomena have three major elements which foster teachers' reflective thinking: cognitive, narrative, and critical. The cognitive element fosters concern regarding broad teaching principles and strategies of classroom management and organization that appear to transcend subject matter (Shulman, 1987). This element coincides with the most personal form of reflective practice--the "inner dialogue" which a teacher has with her/himself. Table 11 presents examples of the teacher's inner dialogue at the elementary cognitive level.

The immediacy of teaching precludes others from participating in reflection-in-action, though the reflective teacher can learn to bring multiple perspectives into this process, as seen in the examples of reflection-in-action from Table 12.

Table 11.

Examples of Teacher's Inner Dialogue in Elementary Cognitive Level

Are all the children following my directions?

Are their eyes all on me?

Do they seem to understand my directions?

Am I missing anything from what I have planned in the written lesson plan?

Do I have to make some changes? Why? Do I want to change?

Table 12.

Examples of Teacher's Reflection-in-Action Inner Dialogue

If I were the child who seems to be having some difficulties following the directions or who seems to have some conflicts with me or other peers, what/how would I feel about this activity/lesson/materials/situation?

What individually appropriate change do I need to make for the child?

Is there any other child who seems to have a problem or difficulty in my lesson ideas/procedures/directions?

What are the needed changes that I have to make in this lesson activity?

The major aspect of the narrative element of reflection is that it serves to contextualize the classroom experience for teachers and *others*, thus providing them with a much richer understanding of what takes place in the classroom and in the teachers' construction of reality (Reagan, 1993). For student teachers, the "others" become the classroom cooperating teacher and university supervisor who work together to present the student teacher with numerous opportunities to reflect upon her or his exhibited practices. Key to the resulting narrative are questions designed to uncover the student teachers' decisions *during* the teaching act. This narrative element of reflection provides one of the more effective ways in which developmentally and culturally appropriate reflective practice can be encouraged: by suggesting that teachers reexamine the classroom phenomena from multiple perspectives. Table 13 provides examples of narrative elements of reflection-on-action in inner dialogue:

Table 13.

Examples of Teacher's Narrative Elements in Reflection-on-Action Inner Dialogue

---

What had happened during the lesson delivery?

What were your unexpected/unprepared experiences during the lesson?

What changes did you make for the unexpected reactions from the children in order for you to provide not only developmentally but also culturally congruent individual learning experiences?

What made you change in that particular way in that situation?

Was it DCAP for the individual child?

After you had made some changes, what differences did you find which would make a better approach than your previously planned one?

How did you know that the children were learning and receiving equal, fair, and congruent learning experience?

These inquiries allow the prospective teachers to be both process and outcome oriented. It helps them to recognize how the decision they make influences the learning that occurs.

Reflection-for-action represents a habit of mind that enables practitioners to call upon what they have learned through their personal (cognitive) and shared (narrative) reflections in a more deliberative sense as they plan future teaching episodes. Ideally, this planning would include a critical element of reflection, often identified with critical pedagogy and pedagogical theory, that prompts teachers to critically analyze different instructional perspectives and to use them to understand and properly act on revealed inconsistencies (McLaren, 1989; Nieto, 1992; Reagan, 1993). Suggested inquiries for this reflection-for-action are in Table 14:

Table 14.
Examples of Critical Elements in Reflection-for-Action Inner Dialogue

---

What did I learn from my previous teaching?

What do I have to prepare or know more about regarding the individual child's unique learning style, communication style, interests, needs, and so on?

How should I extend or change my teaching style, interaction styles, or materials that would affect all learners' development and learning experiences fairly?

What are the critical things that I should consider and prepare for my next lesson that would allow me to fully support and be responsive to the individual learners' developmentally and culturally congruent experience, and that would allow all of us to have an equal and fair learning experience?

This critical element of reflection influences early childhood prospective teachers' developmentally and culturally appropriate practice in light of education that is for all.

Inquiry-Oriented Preparation

Education that is multicultural--for all--seeks to structure schools for equal opportunity, function cross-culturally, and promote a curriculum for knowledge construction which develops the learning communities' intellectual, moral, and social dispositions by providing opportunities for learners to participate in building knowledge and constructing their own interpretations of historical, social, and current events (Banks, 1994a, b).

To reach these goals within a framework for developmentally and

culturally appropriate practice, early childhood prospective teachers must learn to: (1) consider their work in relation to issues of social compassion and justice, (2) focus on both process and outcome, (3) examine classroom phenomena from multiple perspectives, (4) recognize how the decisions they make influence the learning that occurs, and (5) look critically at the ethical bases of what happens in the classroom and determine how their practices affect all learners. At the same time prospective teachers must recognize that while they will always realize a desire to begin at the technical/instrumental stage of reflective practice, DCAP occurs primarily at the dialectical stage by critically thinking about whether every child in the classroom has received an equal and culturally congruent teaching and learning experience for their development. Critical reflection in, on, and for action helps to ensure that teachers consider multiple and diversified viewpoints as well as the long-term social and moral consequences of their decisions. Teaching in this fashion will not only reflect developmentally and culturally appropriate practice with young children, but is more likely to result in education that is truly multicultural--for all (Colton & Sparks-Langer, 1993).

Zeichner's (1981-82) inquiry-oriented approach is an example of a teacher education model that emphasizes the dialectical focus sought in an advanced stage of pedagogical practice (see Table 9). As such, it expands the definition of reflective teaching to include a critical consideration of education that is multicultural (Gore, 1987; Gipe & Richards, 1992). This inquiry-oriented approach emphasizes the preparation of teachers who are both willing and able to reflect on the origins, purposes, and consequences of their instructional actions, as well as on the material and ideological constraints and encouragements embedded in the classroom, school, and societal contexts in which they practice (Zeichner, 1981-82).

Zeichner's approach seeks to enable prospective teachers to become self-directed, individually reflective educators capable of promoting developmentally and culturally appropriate practice toward education that is multicultural. Therefore, an inquiry-oriented approach seems best suited to

help prospective teachers develop insight into how to promote a true equal learning and teaching opportunity for diverse young learners. When prospective teachers are exposed to inquiry-oriented reflective teaching experience as a built-in-procedure in their teacher preparation program-- especially the student teaching supervision of their first novice teaching experience--their interpretation of DCAP can become more self-directed and personally meaningful.

Proposed Model of Inquiry-Oriented
Reflective Supervision for DCAP

The dominant characteristics of clinical supervision (Goldhammer, Anderson, & Krajewski, 1980) can be employed in an inquiry-oriented teacher education model for student teaching--especially within the structure of clinical supervision and its emphasis on classroom instruction (Zeichner & Liston, 1987).

Clinical supervision supports the professional development of teachers by emphasizing classroom instructional practices (Acheson & Gall, 1992). However, clinical supervision must become more reflective in nature if it is to both enhance teaching practice and increase student learning. It must help teachers become more cognizant of their beliefs and values, more self-monitoring and self-analytical concerning their teaching and its impact on learners, and better able to solve the instructional problems that occur naturally in the process of teaching and learning. Reflection, in short, is the driving force behind successful clinical supervision (Nolan & Huber, 1989).

A Cycle of Inquiry-Oriented Reflective Supervision for DCAP

Currently, clinical supervision contains several sequential elements: establishing readiness; pre-observation conference; observation; analysis; post-observation conference; and cycle evaluation (Smyth, 1984; Goldsberry, 1986). Once readiness is established, the subsequent elements

operate to develop nonjudgmental professional relationships between teachers and supervisors (Nolan & Francis, 1992).

The proposed cycle of inquiry-oriented reflective supervision for DCAP incorporates these major elements; however, the crucial element of establishing readiness is expanded to include four sequential components of its own. The following five phases represent a proposed cycle of inquiry-oriented reflective supervision for DCAP.

Phase 1: Self-examination. As the first phase of inquiry-oriented reflective supervision for DCAP, self-examination serves as an important tool to develop one's espoused platforms. Espoused platforms refer to the teacher's beliefs and goals for teaching and learning applied directly to his/her specific teaching situation. Platforms include goals for young children from diverse backgrounds, criteria for appropriate teaching and interaction, expectations for learners, beliefs about subject matter, and recognition of situational influences. In this phase, prospective teachers should reflect upon their own and others' cultures (see Chapter 3, Table 3: Suggested Inquiries for Autobiographical Self-Examination for Diversity). Doing so enables teachers to realize and value the significance of their own individual differences in an effort to enhance their cross-cultural and multicultural sensitivity (Banks, 1994a, b; Locke, 1992; McAdoo, 1993; Nieto, 1992; Sleeter, 1991; Stewart & Bennett, 1991).

This self-examination further allows students to reconnect to what they have learned regarding DCAP and education that is multicultural for all during their teacher preparation coursework. The "Education That Is Multicultural Self-Assessment" framework (see Table 15) can help to promote this reflective reconnection by moving students into the beginning mode of DCAP before encountering their actual lesson or activity development and application for young children.

By carrying out this self-examination process at the outset of student teaching, prospective teachers can be helped to articulate their own espoused platforms. Supervisors need to clearly understand how each student teacher has interpreted education that is multicultural in light of DCAP and to use this information as a knowledge base when developing personal relationships and reviewing student teachers' lesson planning, and helping them to reflect on their actions.

Table 15.

Education That is Multicultural Self-Assessment[7]

(Table 15 continued to p.91)

- Have I had instruction about developmentally appropriate practice, culturally appropriate practice, and education that is multicultural since my introductory course? (If YES, name course and content)

- What are my definitions of developmentally appropriate practice, culturally appropriate practice, and education that is multicultural?

- What kinds of knowledge and experience would I like to promote for children (and their families) in multicultural settings?

- Have I had any assignments or projects that include aspects of education that are multicultural? (If YES, briefly note, including course)

- Have I seen any learning environments that reflected education that is multicultural?
   (If YES, why do I believe that the environment I saw reflected education that is multicultural? If NO, why do I believe that the environment I saw did not reflect it?)

- Have I examined any curriculum materials that I have used in my class or seen in use for multicultural aspects? For bias?

- Have I had experience with adapting different teaching strategies to various learning styles?

- How comfortable do I feel raising questions about multicultural issues in my university classes?

Table 15 Continued

- Has anyone (e.g., professors) tried to help me learn how to incorporate the notion of DCAP for young children into my lesson planning?

- Have I had any discussions about the teacher's role in school-home-community relations?

- Have I had any discussion about test biases or biased assessment tools and approaches?

- Have I had any discussion about the hidden curriculum?

-Have I had any projects or assignments that dealt with the cross-cultural child development, children's play, self-concept, self-esteem, family-esteem, and self-identity in the U.S.?

Phase 2: Reflective Discussion. As a second phase, discuss the student teacher's responses to the questions in Phase 1. Students can share their reflection about the self-assessment by addressing such questions as: "What does the assessment really tell me about myself?" "What types of concerns surfaced as I considered these questions?"

As closure for phase 2, discussion needs to focus on reflection-for-action. Here, supervisors pose probing questions to encourage student teachers' autonomy (Nolan & Huber, 1989). Supervisors might also employ some reality-based cases which present cross-cultural child development, diversified individual needs, or parent expectations toward the school and the early childhood teachers, in order to provide student teachers with a clear sense of how to understand individual cultural differences and how to connect their understandings to DCAP (Merseth, 1991, 1992; Shulman, 1992).

Phase 3: Observation for Exploring Diversity in the Learning Environment. Here, student teachers explore the nature of diversity in the classroom or center in which they have been placed for the practicum. They are encouraged to see and realize what diversity has existed in the classroom, what brings cultural diversity into the classroom, and how they can use this diversity as a learning resource. In addition, student teachers need to look critically at the ethical bases for what happens in the classroom and begin to consider how pedagogical practices successfully and productively affect all young children (Lasley, 1992; Reagan, 1993). During this observation period supervisors need to promote reflective discussions within their seminars in which students not only share their thoughts, but consider what they see in light of technical/instrumental, practical/ conceptual, and critical/dialectical practice (see Table 9).

Phase 4: Planning for Developmentally and Culturally Appropriate Practice. This step allows student teachers to consider strategies to enact DCAP, mentally play them out in their lesson plans, and actually carry them out under inquiry-oriented reflective clinical supervision.

Teachers' decisions made before and after instruction constitute "lesson planning"--one of the most important and fundamental elements in teaching. Acheson and Gall (1992) note that some teachers have difficulty with instruction when they do not plan lessons effectively. Writing structured lesson plans may be a useful starting point for the development of lesson planning skills, but it should not be the only supervision focus. Supervisors must also help prospective teachers to increase the amount of time they spend in reflection-for-action (mental lesson planning) while helping them develop careful, defensible written plans. Table 13 and Table 14 are the suggested inquiries in reflection-on-action and reflection-for-action to promote early childhood education practitioners' mental lesson planning as well as ongoing self-evaluation.

According to Neely (1986) and Morine (1976), reflective lesson planning is an appropriate procedure for stimulating prospective teachers to analyze the mental processes underlying their novice instruction. Within the DCAP model, this is also the time for student teachers to become aware of the types of reflection they experience relative to their developing sense of teaching (see Table 9). Ultimately, self-monitored lesson planning by the student teacher enables her or him to better recognize whether the planning is appropriate for the target children during the actual lesson activity, thus encouraging the habit of reflection-in-action. In this mode the student teachers become as action researchers themselves (Ross, 1989).

Phase 5: Regular Supervision Cycle. In this phase, student teachers and supervisors complete the "clinical" supervision cycle (i.e., pre-observation conference; observation; analysis; post-observation conference; and cycle evaluation). To carry out a genuine inquiry-oriented approach in seeking DCAP, however, supervisors need to continually promote awareness of the diversity represented in the practicum setting by requiring students teachers to exercise their various perspective-taking skills (Chapter 3, Table 5 and 6, for example, they might ask, "what if I use second-person or multiple/multiethnic perspective-taking in that particular situation or conflict? What are the things that I might be able to find out through these various perspective-taking approaches that would help me better understand the diverse children's different needs and to interact with the individual child properly and fairly?"). In this way student teachers can learn to be highly sensitive and flexible with respect to these cultural differences (Grant & Zeichner, 1984; Pajak, 1993). Supervisors must also continuously reinforce the fact that novice teaching is a beginning period for continued learning about teaching and schooling and for establishing pedagogical habits of self-directed growth--sense of self-supervision, rather than solely an official period for the application and demonstration of previously required conventional knowledge and skills (Zeichner & Liston, 1987).

The proposed inquiry-oriented reflective supervision approach for DCAP is designed to promote student teachers' reflection--especially reflection-in-action--so that they can achieve developmentally and culturally congruent and fair educational practices. Though explicated here within a preservice framework, the DCAP model lends itself quite well to an inservice framework. The basic principles and premises can easily be recast in a model designed to introduce and promote DCAP through an extended inservice program coupled with existing clinical supervision efforts in support of practicing teachers' professional development. Staff development efforts like these would not only enhance the educational opportunities of diverse youngsters, they would also assure a proliferation of teachers pursuing developmentally and culturally appropriate practice in their classrooms-- many of whom, in the role of cooperating teacher, would help to better prepare novice early childhood professionals. Indeed, given the heavy reliance on shared and interactive reflection in the preservice model of DCAP, veteran educators who are critically reflective and who attend to students' cultural differences in ways suggested here make ideal partners for the supervision cycle. Additionally, unlike the preservice model that has students "going through" a DCAP-focused program, the professional development model provides the long-term situation required for truly cumulative thought and experience.

This inquiry-oriented reflective supervision model for prospective teachers' field experience has been used empirically. Chapter 6 introduces a research approach exploring how early childhood prospective teachers make sense of DCAP in the classroom using this supervision model. Chapter 7 discusses the results and implication of the study.

Chapter Six

Making Sense of Developmentally and Culturally Appropriate Practice with Prospective Teachers in the Classroom

Research Backgrounds and Questions

In Chapter 6 and Chapter 7, I introduce the novice early childhood teachers' DCAP teaching experiences. This phenomenological study explores prospective early childhood teachers' conceptualization and practical sense making of developmentally and culturally appropriate practice in their first teaching experience.

The following question was the main point of investigation for this study: How do early childhood education preservice teachers understand, account for, and incorporate DCAP in their teaching lives? Related questions included: (1) In what ways do prospective teachers, who commit themselves to practice early childhood education that is multicultural, incorporate DCAP into their lesson planning and implementation? and (2) What are the obstacles that prospective teachers perceive and experience as they strive to implement their understanding of developmentally and culturally appropriate practice in their teaching?

This study is based on the theoretical framework of social phenomenology. Social phenomenology enables qualitative researchers to explore human consciousness via the ways that the life world--experiential world every person takes for granted--is produced and experienced by members (Schultz, 1970; Holstein & Gubrium, 1994). Social phenomenologists see that individuals construct and reconstruct their unique understanding of reality, which is considered intersubjectivity. This intersubjectivity then becomes objectified as the experiential world that every person takes for granted. Multiple ways of interpreting objectified intersubjectivities are available to constitute reality (Bogdan & Bicklen, 1992). This theoretical framework enabled me to explore the ways that early childhood preservice teachers in this study formed their DCAP consciousness and used DCAP in their teaching experience in various ways. This theoretical framework also allowed for the research participants to share how they came to understand, account for, and incorporate their concepts of DCAP into their teaching lives.

Research Methods

The Context for the Study

The participants[8] of this study consisted of early childhood preservice teachers who were enrolled in Clinical Application of Instruction in Early Childhood Education (CI495) during the Spring semester 1995, at Pennsylvania State University. I was instructor and supervisor of the course. My major role in this study was as a participant observer. As both course instructor and researcher in the study, I made decisions that ultimately affected the evolution of the course and the research purpose; that is, which participants to select, where to focus my questions at the interview, where to focus during observation of their teaching, and what data to select.

This course, taken the semester prior to student teaching, provides with prospective teachers an opportunity to make a connection between their teacher preparation courses and actual implementation of their own learning in the field. The most significant aspect of this course is that the prospective teachers have their first novice teaching experience. The course provides opportunities for prospective teachers to reflect on what they have been learning about DCAP in previous coursework, how they make sense of DCAP, how they implement their conceptions of DCAP into actual lesson planning and instruction, and how they evaluate their first DCAP teaching experience. Each preservice student teacher was expected to: (1) attend weekly two-hour seminars for fifteen weeks; (2) spend one half-day and one full day per week in an early childhood setting; (3) write a reflective journal entry focusing on a journal assignment for each day of field experience and seminar; (4) develop and implement ten lesson plans; (5) complete two of the inquiry-oriented reflective DCAP supervision cycles (see Chapter Five); and (6) participate in the mid-term and final self-evaluation conferences, which were conducted as semi-structured interviews.

Establishing Readiness

When I first met my prospective research participants in the field experience class, I presented my two-page research proposal and research consent form that had been approved by the Office of Human Research Subjects at Pennsylvania State University. I explained the nature of the study. Everybody in the class agreed to participate in the study.

The second week of the seminar, I discussed each school site that the students could select for placement for their field experience, including the major characteristics of each school program (e.g., open-ended, Montessori, and traditional kindergarten); characteristics of the school population; cooperating teachers' professional characteristics (such as proficiency in parents involvement, anti-bias education, multicultural early childhood education, or loving and caring for young children), name, years of experience as a cooperating teacher with this field experience, address, and telephone number.

Then I allowed my students to select the school setting for their field experience. After they decided on the school, I gave them two weeks to visit and observe the school and the cooperating teacher and her interaction with children. Then, the third or fourth week of the semester, the prospective teachers made their final decision regarding their placement for this field experience.

I considered the students' personal needs when facilitating their placement in the best possible and professional way I could. I tried not to direct them for their placement. I gave them considerable information and a time to observe the actual school and cooperating teacher before they made their decision on their placement. During this time, I carefully observed each individual regarding what and how they made their decision. The two participants' stories of choosing a school for their prepracticum are presented in Chapter 7.

My basic criteria for selecting a classroom as a school site for my preservice student teachers were to have: (1) a full-time classroom teacher with more than three years of teaching experience who knows about Developmentally Appropriate Practice, and (2) to have children from diverse backgrounds based on family structures and environment, race, ethnicity, language, gender, and special needs.

Data Collection Methods and Procedures

The data sources for this study were: audiotapes of weekly seminar discussions; personal documents, such as reflective journals, autobiographical self-examination to promote diversity (Chapter 3, Table 3) and multicultural needs assessments (Chapter 5, Table 15); lesson plans; field notes from my observations of the preservice teachers' field experience; and semi-structured tape-recorded interviews.

Weekly Seminar

There were two hours of seminar discussion every week for 15 weeks. The seminar was designed for the students to share their overall issues on their first teaching experience and understanding of DCAP. I facilitated the seminar discussion based on the concerns the prospective teachers brought with them to class.

My major role for facilitating the seminar discussion was as participant observer. I always carefully observed the moment the participants voluntarily brought their own issues of DCAP into the session. I helped them discuss their issues by posing divergent, probing questions which focused on my research purpose, such as:

> *How did you come to understand DCAP by implementing your own lesson?*
> *How did you come to understand DCAP by observing your cooperating or other peer teachers?*
> *How did you come to understand DCAP by observing the children's play behavior and interaction with others?*
> *In what ways did your lesson activity for young children support your own ways of DCAP?*

Each participant was also encouraged to react to the seminar discussion in their academic journal, which was collected every week during the semester.

During the fourth and fifth weeks of the semester, the preservice student teachers explored the nature of diversity in the classroom in which they had been placed for the field experience. They were encouraged to see and realize what diversity existed in the classroom, what brought cultural diversity into the children's play, and how they could use this diversity as a rich learning resource.

In order to facilitate their observation and the discussion after the observation, I, as participant observer, provided several questions which helped them to look critically at the ethical bases of what happened in the classroom, and in what ways these happenings affected each individual child's learning and development, and his/her life in the classroom. The actual inquiries that I used for this phase were the following:

> How was the classroom observation?...What have you discovered about the classroom?...What type of diversity exists in the classroom?...What was your discovery of diverse children's play?

What was your discovery of each individual child's characteristics of learning and development?...What makes you think that each individual has his or her own characteristics of learning and development?...What makes you think that the individual child's characteristics bring diversity into their play phenomena and the classroom culture?... In what ways did the classroom environment and the teachers support each child's unique needs for his/her own learning and development?... How was the classroom culture?... Was the classroom culture fair to all children?...If it is a fair/unfair/unhealthy classroom culture, what leads you to think in that way?... In what sense does the classroom teacher's practice support/not support DCAP?... What alternative ways would you like to try for your own DCAP teaching, based on your observation?... (Field Note, Seminar 4, February 2, 1995).

After the seminar, the prospective teachers were encouraged to reflect on their classroom observation and seminar discussion in their academic journal.

I audiotaped each seminar discussion to further my reflective field note-taking as a researcher. Right after each seminar, I spent at least one hour summarizing the seminar discussion, particularly focusing on the prospective teachers' self-expression that seemed to relate to their DCAP. Whenever I felt that my memory was not clear, or that it was important to record exactly what the prospective teachers said, I listened to the audiotape to clarify my field notes.

Reflective Academic Journal

A reflective academic journal entry was collected from the prospective teachers each week. My analysis of personal documents and reflective journals provided an unobtrusive measure (Bodgan & Biklen, 1992) of the participants' understanding, conceptualization, and their thinking about DCAP. The prospective teachers were encouraged to use guidelines for the journal assignment which were included in their course syllabus. These guidelines were designed to encourage more of an in-depth self-reflection on their first teaching experience and their DCAP teaching life.

When I reviewed reflective journals, I provided some probing and open-ended questions or some comments on several aspects:

> (1) different aspects of young children's play and their developmental changes - *How did you know the children were learning/ understanding the concept?*
>
> (2) diversity among young children's learning - *How did the children react to the materials/topic?, How is each child's understanding of his/her own learning different? Can we think about what makes them different?*
>
> (3) the prospective teacher's pedagogical concerns about DCAP - *In what ways does your DCAP lesson properly respond to each individual child's meaningful play and learning experiences so that everybody has an equal and congruent learning experience?*

Autobiographical Self-Examination for Diversity and Multicultural Needs Self-Assessments

In the second week of the seminar, I collected two personal essays from the student teachers, "Autobiographical Self-Examination for Diversity" (see Chapter 3, Table 3) and "Education That Is Multicultural Self-Assessment" (Chapter, 5 Table 15), which I had developed for their self-examination as an important tool to develop their espoused platforms for DCAP. The preservice teachers in the course had a week to do personal reflective writing based on the questions from these forms. They were encouraged to think and respond to as many questions as possible, but responding to all the questions was not required. These data helped me to understand my participants' prior knowledge and their understanding of self and the issue of DCAP. I used these two personal documents as important pieces of information for the data triangulation in order to verify the categories I discovered from each of the final participants.

At the third seminar, the participants engaged in a 30-40 minute small-group discussion and then a 30-40 minute general group discussion to share their experience of autobiographical self-examination based on the essay assignment. As participant observer during the last part of the discussion in the seminar, I focused on each participant's self-realization for DCAP as a prospective early childhood teacher. The main inquiries that I posed in this phase were:

> *How well do I know my own culture?*
> *In what ways did/does my culture(s) help me to become an early*
> *childhood teacher who can provide an equal and congruent learning*
> *experience for all children?*
> *How well do I understand education that is truly multicultural to*
> *promote a culturally congruent and equal learning environment for all*
> *the children I will teach?*

After the seminar, all the participants were required to reflect on the seminar discussion and express their thoughts in their journals about the meaning of autobiographical self-awareness as a means for developing sensitivity for diversity.

Lesson Planning

At the fifth seminar, we discussed child's play-based lesson planning that is appropriate for the young children's learning experiences. The prospective teachers were encouraged to create and use their own written lesson plan format. I also suggested that they talk with me about their written or mental lesson plan each time they developed one.

Written lesson plans were collected starting the sixth week of field experience. Each week the prospective teachers were required to complete at least one lesson plan in advance for the following week of teaching. I suggested that my students also get other teachers' points of view regarding their lesson ideas (for example, cooperating teachers or supervisor, or other peer teachers). Sometimes cooperating teachers gave them practical ideas that the prospective teachers had not thought about for the children in that particular classroom. However, it was their decision alone as to whether to follow the others' suggestions or not. I mentioned to them, "If you decide to follow others' suggestions, you might also think about in what ways the suggested ideas will support your DCAP teaching life" (field note, February 23, 1995).

I reviewed either their written or mental lesson plan and offered some probing questions for them to make sense of DCAP before they taught the actual lesson. The most common questions that I used in this phase were:

> *In what sense is this play-based activity/lesson age-appropriate?*
> *In what ways can your lesson procedures support individual learning characteristics?*
> *In what ways do these lesson procedures help the children's culturally congruent learning experience?*

Participant Observation and Supervision of the Field Experience

Participant observation took placed during the supervision of each prospective teacher in her field placement. I provided pre-conferences for anybody at any time by their request and observed at least two of the ten lessons that they taught. At the pre-conference, I indirectly helped the student teachers focus on certain instructional aspects of their DCAP mental lesson plan.

The most common inquiries that I used during pre-conference were:

> *Can you tell me about your lesson? What will the lesson be like? Do the lesson activity ideas and approaches support your DCAP? How?*
> *How would you like to go about helping each child understand the lesson ideas or the concept that you want them to learn about?*
> *What were the prerequisite knowledge/concepts that each child needs to have before this lesson in order for them to have a culturally congruent learning experience?*
> *How do you know all children have this prerequisite knowledge for this lesson?*

I also facilitated them in thinking about what issues they wished me to observe as supervisor that would help their own sense making of DCAP teaching. My field notes were used for recording the story of these pre-conferences.

Following each pre-conference was the actual observation of the lesson in class. During the prospective teacher's lessons, I observed various aspects, including some specific issues that they had requested me to observe. My field notes were constantly used to describe the setting that I observed; the activities that took place in that setting, the children who participated in the lesson activities, and other emerging issues for the study.

A follow-up post-conference was held at which time I suggested that the prospective teacher evaluate his/her own DCAP lesson plan and implementation using her/his own reflection-on-action. As participant observer of this study, I provided some probing inquiries focusing on how the teacher made sense of DCAP as actually used in a lesson activity. The most common inquiries that I used for this phase were the suggested inquiries for reflection-on-action in Chapter 5, Table 13:

What had happened during the lesson delivery?
What were your unexpected/unprepared experiences during the lesson?
What changes did you make for the unexpected reactions from the children in order for you to provide not only developmentally but also culturally congruent individual learning experiences?
What made you change in that particular way in that situation?
Was it DCAP for the individual child?
After you had made some changes, what differences did you find which would make a better approach than your previously planned one?
How did you know that the children were learning and receiving an equal, fair and congruent learning experience?
In what ways did your written or mental lesson preparation help you?
What was the best/worst moment of your DCAP teaching during the lesson? Why?

As a final step in the supervision and observation cycle, I suggested that the prospective teachers write a reflective self-evaluation about their own DCAP lesson planning and its implementation in their journal. After each lesson, the preservice teachers were also encouraged to do post-lesson planning by reviewing the original lesson plan. They were required to do a self-reflective lesson evaluation on the back side of the original lesson plan. In this phase they were going through reflection-for-action using the suggested inquiries in Chapter 5, Table 14:

> *What did I learn from my previous teaching?*
> *What more do I have to know about the individual child's unique learning style, communication style, interests, needs etc.?*
> *How/what should I extend/change my teaching style, interaction styles, as well as materials that would affect all learners' development and learning experiences fairly?*
> *What are the critical things that I should consider and prepare for my next class that would allow me to fully support and be responsible to the individual learners' developmentally and culturally congruent experience and which will allow all of us to have an equal and fair learning experience?*

Semi-Structured Interviews

For mid-term and final evaluation of the field experience, I used semi-structured interviews. Semi-structured interviews were developed based on each prospective teacher's reflection on DCAP so that the interviews of all the prospective teachers were somewhat systematic for my research purpose.

The mid-term interview enabled me to complete the search for my final participants, develop and sequence questions, and make decisions as to what areas to pursue in greater depth at a later observation and final interview. Each interview with the participants was tape recorded and transcribed. With the transcribed data of two interviews of each person, I attempted to see how they formed their concept of DCAP during their novice teaching. In the following section, I describe my procedures for selecting the two final participants for this study.

Purposeful Sampling for Research Participants

This phenomenological research was a highly exploratory study to describe and analyze how early childhood prospective teachers who have committed themselves to practice DCAP during field experience made sense of what it means to implement DCAP. To select information-rich data for an in-depth study of the prospective teachers' response to and use of DCAP, I incorporated an ongoing purposeful sampling procedure into my research (Patton, 1990; Merriam, 1988).

The purposeful sampling procedure helped me to identify persons in the course who showed personal interest in making sense of DCAP in their first teaching experience. I started with all sixteen preservice student teachers who were enrolled in the course and voluntarily agreed to participate in the study. Throughout the major data collection, using my field notes, I kept a frequency record of times they reflected on DCAP. It was based on each participant's self-exploration regarding his/her understanding of DCAP and self-awareness of DCAP in lesson planning and implementation, or obstacles encountered in his/her DCAP. For example:

> I always make my lesson multicultural...I ask them question, that pertain to their native country and things like that (Irene's mid-term conference interview, March 20, 1995).

> The key to developing lessons for my DCAP is to choose the content that enables young children to explore their own direct experiences of diverse learning; in ways that connect to each of their individual needs (Mindy's journal entry 7, February 16, 1995).

> To me, lesson planning for DCAP means creating lessons that are "naturally" appropriate based on the ages, developmental levels, and backgrounds of the children. The DCAP content in the lessons should not be overt; it should be inherent in all of the lessons, but there should not be direct attention paid to it. The planning for DCAP takes careful consideration and creativity-how to get the message across without saying, "Here is the DCAP part of the lesson." Right now, I am not sure I know how to plan for DCAP, but I am sure I will when

I begin my lesson planning for my center (Sharon's journal entry 5,
February 9, 1995).

Each time I saw these issues in their data (in their academic reflective
journal, lesson plans, seminar discussion, or interview conference), I
recorded it in my field notes to ascertain who was consistently using and
evaluating DCAP. Therefore, my major concern for an ongoing purposeful
sampling procedure was to find continuity in each participant's voluntary
reflection on his/her DCAP.

Until mid-term, most participants' self-expression of DCAP through
their journals, seminar participation, or interviews was very infrequent. If
they did make a comment, it was more like something they copied from a
literature selection, or they gave their reflection simply because this course
encouraged them to think about DCAP. However, by the end of the
semester, I was able to identify two participants (Ana and Carrie)[9] who
continuously dealt with their own approach to DCAP the entire semester
during the data collection period. Numerous self-expressions about their
DCAP teaching lives were revealed through lesson plans/implementation and
self-evaluation, academic journals, interviews, and my field notes. Their
voices gave me enough information to explore indepth and better understand
DCAP sense making phenomena. Therefore, I selected Carrie and Ana as
the final research participants for my indepth study.

Analysis Techniques

Miles and Huberman (1994) indicate that the researcher must
complete a process that involves reducing the data and manipulating the data
to discover categories. In this study, I present the techniques and methods
I used to ensure the integrity, validity, and accuracy of the data that led to
findings in my qualitative study, using the theoretical framework of social
phenomenology. I also present details of my decision making on data
analysis procedures to support my research credibility.

As I finalized my two major research participants from four months of purposeful sampling procedures, I began to read and analyze my data more in-depth. During this time I attempted to capture descriptive accounts of early childhood education prospective teachers' sense making of DCAP through various data collection strategies.

To complete my data analysis, I continued ongoing readings of journal entries, personal documents, lesson plans, and interview transcriptions. I used field notes to refer to my research experiences with individual students, seminars, and data analysis. Open coding, axial coding, and selective coding were my main data analysis techniques. Along with these coding techniques, selecting significant units, categorizing, memoing, and reflective note-taking were used from the very beginning as important parts of this qualitative research process (Strauss & Corbin, 1990).

During my entire reading of data using the three coding techniques, I looked for emerging patterns and regularities (LeCompt & Preissle, 1993). As patterns and regularities emerged, I recorded them in my field notes and used them later for more in-depth data analysis procedures, such as triangulation of data, in order to verify my discoveries. Because, as a social phenomenologist, I believe our minds continuously construct and reconstruct reality in the process of categorizing and interpreting what we see, hear, and read, I did an informal mental analysis throughout the research process. At the same time, I recorded my mental construction of the data in my field notes, using them as a piece of information for triangulation if these appeared to be a pattern from the data.

After numerous readings during four months of data collection, I went through three major coding systems on each of the participant's, based on Strauss and Corbin's (1990) open, axial, and selective coding (see Table 16). During this period of data analysis, I was careful to maintain a continuous decision-making process of data analysis through readings of the two participants' data in order to have research credibility.

From my field notes, I discovered that I had gone through identical data analysis procedures and techniques in a consistent way with my two participants' data. Table 16 presents the summary of my data analysis based on characteristics of each procedure and the decisions I made.

Open Coding

Open coding is the process of breaking down, examining, comparing, conceptualizing, and categorizing data (Straus & Corbin, 1990). I used this coding system as the first procedure for my data analysis of each participant's conceptual world of DCAP.

Step 1 After numerous readings of the data, I was able to focus on what the participants' were saying that seemed related to my study purpose. In order to easily and visually focus on their particular voices, I decided to use two different colored markers: blue for the participant's voice and orange for my voice (my comments or questions). This simple technique helped me more easily focus on the data.

Step 2 After reading the highlighted part in the original data two or three times, I was able to select and bracket some significant units such as words, phrases, or sentences that seemed to focus on my research issue. I also decided to number each significant unit so that later, when I related each unit's cards, I could still relocate them in their original context.

Step 3 After I bracketed the numerous significant units to do a technical qualitative data analysis, I cut apart one copy of the field notes, personal documents, interview transcripts and journals, placing them on 5x8-inch index cards and coding them to reflect one or more categories. At this step, I also made three additional technical decisions: (1) to have a different color for each participant's cards identification (pink for Ana and green for Carrie); (2) to give a number to each card identification; and (3) to reread the original research question, and make an identification number for the major issues of my research question, and to use the number for briefly relating each significant unit to the research issue (see Table 17).

Using four different identification techniques, including the technique that I made at the open coding step 2, helped me to easily identify each participant's voice, where the incident came from, which issue seemed related to each incident, and even the time the incident occurred during the data collection.

Step 4 The first brief categorization had occurred. By ongoing reading of each card, I could find a significant unit that seemed more like a pattern than the previous step. I transferred patterns and regularities into categories (LeCompt & Preissle, 1993). I made numerous memos of this brief categorization. I could begin to see tentative key concepts that each participant had. In my field notes, I recorded the brief emerging categories from the tentative key concepts. Each person's first brief categories showed more than 70 categories.

Step 5 Obviously, more than 70 categories for each person were too many, although I could see that some categories looked like subcategories of a broader concept, which meant that I needed to further refine the categories to find a category that could combine those subcategories. In this step, I revisited the original data often to get a clear sense of each incident's context, which led me to construct broader categories. For example, in Ana's case, time, efforts, teacher commitment, and effective teacher were emergent tentative categories from the previous open coding step. During Step 5, I put these four together into a broader category termed "effective teacher." After this open coding process, the number of emergent categories dropped dramatically to 22-27 categories for each of the two participants.

Step 6 After the categorization in the previous step, when I revisited the data, I was able to reconstruct my previous categories in greater abstraction. Table 18 shows how I came up with a larger abstract category while still maintaining the meaning of subcategories. By going through this process, I was able to see each participant's major conceptual world of DCAP.

Table 16.

Three-Step Data Analysis Procedures, Techniques Used, and Time Table Two Subjects (Table 16 continued to p.113)

Coding	Characteristics	Techniques Used	Ana	Carrie
Open coding Step 1	The primitive stage. After numerous readings of each set of data, identified physical locations of voices that seemed related to my research issues.	Used two different colored markers to highlight the part that seemed related to my research issues. One was for researcher's voice, the other for the participant's voice.	Countless hours	Countless hours
Step 2	After 2-3 times reading the highlighted parts in the data, selected and bracketed some words, phrases, or sentences that focused on my research issues.	Bracketed all the significant units (words, phrases, sentences) and decided to use numbers to identify original data resources.	About 6.5 hours	About 7 hours
Step 3	After bracketing numerous significant units, cut and placed each of them on an individual card.	Chose different colors for each individual and numbers to identify each card and numbers for relating to research issues.	About 8 hours 123 cards	About 9.5 hours 115 cards

Cording Continued	Characteristics Continued	Techniques Used Continued	Ana Continued	Carrie Continued
Open Coding Step 4	The first brief categorization: finding patterns based on person's words or phases that seemed a key concept.	Sorted cards based on key words or phrases, noted key words and the number to identify the card on the field note.	About 6 hours 70 categories	About 6 hours 80 categories
Step 5	Redefined sub-categories into broader categories	Reviewed all the categories and made some connection with small categories to find broader abstract categories.	About 2 hours 22 categories	About 2 hours 26 categories
Step 6	Reviewed the latest categories and looked for a broader, more abstract word that would combine subcategories.	Drew a simple map of major emergent categories.	About 1.5 hours 5 major categories	About 2 hours 5 major categories

Cording Continued	Characteristics Continued	Techniques Used Continued	Ana Continued	Carrie Continued
Axial Coding	A set of procedures whereby data are put back together in new ways. After open coding, I revisited my original research questions to put back the categories in new ways that would relate to my research issues.	Based on my research issues, puting the data back in five different ways: 1. self-awareness; 2. DCAP understanding 3. lesson planning & implementation; 4. obstacles, 5. reflection on supervision cycle. Resorted the data based on these five issues and finding major categories under these issues.	About 4.5 hours	About 5 hours
Selective Coding	The process of selecting the core categories, systematically relating them to other categories, validating those relations, and filling in categories that need further refinement and development.	It emerged in the midst of axial coding. I was also able to draw core categories systematically relating them to other categories.	About 6 hours issue1: 1 issue2: 4 issue3: 6 issue4: 1 issue5: 1 categories	About 9 hours issue1: 1 issue2: 5 issue3: 3 issue4: 1 issue5: 1 categories

Table 17
Techniques for Card Identification

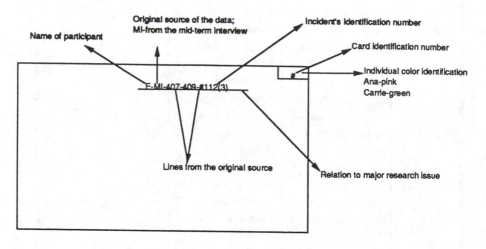

Table 18.
Conceptual Construction Process of Categorization: Ana's Case

Initial category	Sub-category	Final category
parent, family culture, and home culture		
individual uniqueness & needs	*Identity*	
one's own background		
		Respect
similarities/differences		
acceptance	*Acceptance*	
young children's capability & potential		

After these six steps of open coding, I found simple conceptual understanding of DCAP of my two participants.

Axial Coding

Axial coding is a set of procedures whereby data are put back together in new ways (Strauss & Corbin, 1990). After six steps of open coding, I was able to see what made up each person's conceptual world of DCAP. However, I was unclear about how their conceptual world could answer my research questions. Putting data back together in new ways based on my research issues really helped me to clearly discover the phenomena of my research questions.

For this coding procedure, I felt that I needed to go back and reread my original research question. Doing so guided me to begin axial coding, which enabled me to put the data into new modes that related to my research issues.

The large quantity of data became more manageable. I could clearly see how each participant made sense of herself as an early childhood teacher committed to DCAP, how she developed a lesson for DCAP and actually used it, and what obstacles she faced in her DCAP teaching world. This kind of sense making of my data did not clearly occur during the open coding period; it emerged during the axial coding. This kind of coding also led me to illustrate a systematic relationship between categories that I had discovered during the open coding period. These connections on the map led to selective coding.

Selective Coding

Selective coding is the process of selecting the core categories, systematically relating them to other categories, validating those relations, and filling in categories that need further refinement and development (Straus & Corbin, 1990). Selective coding came very naturally during the middle stage of the axial coding, which helped me find core categories of my research issues. In the section of results and discussion in Chapter 7, I present these categories.

Methods for Verification

Using open, axial, and selective coding procedures for this analysis enabled me to compare categories derived through analysis of other data. Through these data analysis techniques, I was able to triangulate the data to provide a richer understanding the participants' conceptualization and sense making of DCAP.

According to Patton (1990), triangulation is one way to cross-check accuracy of data collected. Also, LeCompte and Preissle (1993) note, "Triangulation prevents the researcher from accepting too readily the validity of initial impressions; it enhances the scope, density, and clarity of constructs developed during the course of investigation" (p.48). Triangulation actually happened during my selective coding period. The process of selecting the core categories led me to relate other categories that had been discovered from our initial open coding, my field notes, the raw data of personal documents, lesson planning, reflective journals, and interview transcripts to validate these relationships. I was able to see each participant's conceptual world of DCAP. In addition, to find and present truthful categories on the phenomena of the preservice teachers' conceptualization and sense making of DCAP, I had three colleagues who helped me make proper judgment on the categorization of the data: a Ph.D. candidate who was doing her dissertation study on education that is multicultural in teacher education; the other was a Ph.D. candidate in foreign language education who was doing her dissertation study on teacher beliefs with participants from diverse backgrounds; the third was a professional editor who has her master's degree in English with multicultural teaching experience at the college level.

Chapter Seven

Results, Reality, and Debate

The results of this study offer important findings of early childhood prospective teachers' understanding of developmentally and culturally appropriate practice, and hence have implications for the preparation of early childhood teachers. This chapter contains the stories of the two participants selected for the study.

Phenomena in Ana's DCAP Sense Making

Ana's mother is from a middle-class, suburban, White-American background, and her father is from a lower-class, urban, African-American background. She mentioned that her background helped her to look at things more critically in her education. Ana's critical awareness made her question fairness and truth for all people and made her interested in anti-bias education in early childhood education. She believes an anti-bias curriculum enhances young children's critical thinking and problem solving skills. Later in her DCAP study, she reflected on the anti-bias approach:

> Because of the traditional curriculum in the schools, I was always being made aware of discrepancies in what I was taught [at school] and what I know from my family history. I suppose this may not have always helped me socially because I often got into heated discussions about the materials [for example textbooks], but I strongly believe that my background has always helped me to look at things more critically

when it comes to my education. I often ask myself questions like: Is this fair/true for all people? Does this coincide with what I know to be true in my life? (Ana's autobiography, p.1, January 1995).

...Since I like to teach critical thinking to young children, I am very interested in anti-bias curriculum and multicultural education (field note, third seminar discussion, January 1995).

Ana wants to be an early childhood teacher who teaches children respect for and appreciation of others as part of multicultural early childhood education. She explained as follows:

I want to be a teacher because of my feelings of respect for the profession and my dedication to change the world from the ground up. If America and the rest of the world is going to be a healthy and happy environment for all of its inhabitants, the education system is going to have to change pretty drastically. Young children need to be taught respect for, appreciation of, and knowledge about all people and things (Ana's autobiography, p.2, January 1995).

As Kincheloe (1993) has noted, the background and expectations of the observer shape people's perceptions of education. This is true of Ana.

The autobiographical self-awareness activity presented at the beginning of this field experience was a meaningful experience for Ana. She considered it as an extremely important awareness experience which would help her to be an effective teacher who practices fairness in education. Ana indicated that without understanding oneself, teachers are risking being unfair to their students. By going through an in-depth exploration of self-identity, she believed that we could be more open-minded:

Last week's seminar concerning our autobiographical self-awareness was quite eye-opening... It is extremely important to be knowledgeable about one's own background in order to be an effective teacher...I think it is also important to know yourself, so that you can acknowledge where you are coming from. I think that

people's thought process are determined by their culture... Without
recognizing where one's coming from, a teacher is not being fair to
his/her students... I want to also stress the importance of other
cultures. By being proud of the group(s) that you belong to, you
should always leave room for other cultures to be appreciated... By
doing this, we cannot help but be more open-minded about others
regardless of the color of their skin, the language that they speak, or
where their great-grandparents lived (Ana's journal entry 3, January
1995).

Ana liked the fact that this field experience and seminar were
designed for her to grow in not only developmentally but also culturally
appropriate pedagogical practice:

I am glad that this course emphasizes this kind of issue as DCAP for
my actual teaching experience during my teacher preparation. Because
personally I truly believe in education that is multicultural (field note,
seminar 2, Ana's comment, January 19, 1995).

As indicated by the above quote, as early as the second seminar
class, Ana articulated a strong commitment to DCAP. For this reason, Ana
was a prime candidate for study. The remainder of this section chronicles
the ways in which Ana continued to make sense of DCAP over the course
of the semester.

Field Placement

Ana wanted to have a teaching experience at Home for Children[10],
a day care center in State College, since she knew about its program and a
cooperating teacher from one of her previous early childhood education
courses. During the course, the cooperating teacher from Home for Children
came to the class and talked about the school's philosophy and her personal
teaching practices. The teacher had eighteen years of teaching experience
and seven years as a cooperating teacher. This teacher emphasized and
practiced anti-bias curriculum and education that is multicultural. Ana said

that she really enjoyed the cooperating teacher's introduction to the program and that she had even observed this teacher's classroom and really liked the classroom environment (field note, conference with Ana for her placement, January 23, 1995). During Ana's field experience, the classroom had seven ethnically diverse children among a total of fifteen students.

From my interaction with Ana, it was clear that her understanding of DCAP started with a strong interest in anti-bias curriculum and education that is multicultural. She obviously recognized that Home for Children would provide her learning opportunities in these areas:

> I was quite pleased with my experience at Home for Children. While the physical environment is, admittedly, not the best that I have ever seen, it is appropriate and pleasurable for the student...The center's philosophy includes critical thinking, problem solving and cooperation...They allow and expect the students to arrive at a solution that both parties agree to...All cultures are actively celebrated in the curriculum. The student population is very diverse (racially, linguistically and ethnically) and this diversity is reflected in the books, the food, the language, the holidays, and the activities that are taught. Their treatment of cultures other than American is full of acceptance instead of tokenization. During calendar and song time, children ask to sing and count in several (I think it's seven) different languages; children that aren't native English speakers are talked to, as much as possible, in their native tongue. Less than half of the books that I have noticed on the bookshelf primarily deal with White-American children or families. The physical environment is overflowing with representations of different types of people and languages (e.g., puzzles, posters, games, and toys). Every holiday, whether it is religious or cultural, is discussed at its appropriate time. The four teachers at Home for Children take concrete steps towards learning about different cultures, especially trying to learn about the different cultures in the classroom. There are children from Holland, Saudi Arabia, Korea, England. Most of these children have an extremely hard time each morning when their mom/dad leaves. They cry and usually need to be held by one of the teachers. The problem is that it is rather hard to console a child without being able to verbally communicate with him/her. One of the ways that they are

dealing with this problem is that the teachers are trying to learn key phrases in the child's native language. There are sheets posted all over the center with appropriate phrases like "Mommy will be back later this afternoon," or "Do you have to go to the bathroom?" written in both languages (Ana's journal entry 5, p.2, February 1995).

Because the cooperating teacher was committed to both developmentally and culturally appropriate practices in representing the diverse student population at center, this seemed to be a rich environment for a preservice teacher like Ana to make sense of DCAP. Fuller (1992) suggests that placement has an influence on the prospective teacher's learning about teaching in a culturally diverse classroom. Ana's placement was an important influence on her DCAP understanding and experience of diversity.

Ana's Sense Making of DCAP

Several major categories were discovered from data analysis of Ana's work. First, it was teachable moments that governed the way Ana prepared for and implemented her DCAP lessons over the course of the entire semester.

The concept of teachable moments is, in my opinion, as effective (if not more effective) than lesson planning. As education majors, we often give lip service to discovery learning and different learning styles and rates, but then we turn around and plan lessons that direct students' learning in one manner, at one rate and towards one concept. As I learn more about the teachers, practice in the school, I am much more inclined to break away from this stifling way of thinking and teaching at the day care level. Children should not be pushed to learn something that they are not interested in or individually ready for; however, teachers too often force feed students by teaching them meaningless, uninteresting concepts that are too advanced. It is totally against my idea of DCAP...I allow every child to proceed at a rate that is natural for him/her. I use teachable moments, usually individually or with small groups, that slightly build upon knowledge that has been demonstrated through the child's chosen activities (Ana's journal entry 7, February 1995).

> I guess anything about lesson planning for culturally appropriate I
> think it's, it's really hard for teachers to do it, because I never learned
> about how to do it...I believe through teachable moments I can create
> a proper DCAP lesson for young children...in order to create DCAP
> lesson in teachable moments I have to always be trying to learn about
> all different children. It's just hard but I know it's something to help
> us to lead us in the right direction...But it's hard (Ana's mid-term
> interview, March 1995).

Ana expressed strong concern that her teacher preparation program had focused mainly on how to develop a formal lesson plan rather than how to prepare a lesson from a child-initiated, play-based, teachable moment. Ana felt that formal written lesson planning would make the teacher educate children in only one way. It would limit DCAP as diverse learning and teaching.

> ...the concept of DCAP is founded in providing all children with an
> education that is appropriate for her age, her culture, and herself.
> There is no typical child that a teacher can blindly plan all lessons
> around--all children are unique. It's a shame that for the majority of
> America's history [we] have been teaching to only one type of child
> (i.e., the "normal" White child) (Ana's journal entry 4, p.1, January
> 1995).

Hence, so as not to stifle the prospective teacher's developing understanding of DCAP, early childhood teacher preparation for DCAP needs to provide prospective teachers with various ways of developing lesson planning and give prospective teachers various understandings and ideas of teaching.

Second, the main reason that Ana disagreed with using a formal lesson plan and implementation in her DCAP was her discovery of individual difference and respect for it in the classroom:

... Because I don't see children as any children, even children that
look alike on the surface, as being, you know, all together similar that
there's something different and there's something different in every
child that you have to respect and address in your DCAP lesson. And
if it's their family life or if it's how they approach situations or
whatever it is, you have to always be aware of it and be ready to help
them develop their own individuality (Ana's mid-term Interview,
March 1995).

Because of individuality, Ana understood that DCAP allows children
to put their ideas into their lessons so that they can create their own
meaningful learning experiences by themselves. For example, she explained:

I ask the kids, "Is there another way you want to count? What
language?" They have Spanish, Haiti [Creole], Arabic, Korean,
Siamese, Japanese, and French...They say, well "What can we do
about it?" "What do you think?" And the solutions always come from
the children... (Ana's mid-term interview, March 1995).

Respecting young children by incorporating their ideas, their voices, and
their culture into their learning and using their diverse languages illustrate
Ana's respect for individual differences in her DCAP lesson implementation.

In many cases, Ana focused on children's oral expression of their
ideas and feelings in her DCAP as a way to respect the child. She tried to
listen to children's expressions and verbally respond to the child. She
described her practice in seminar observations:

...ask them to verbally say what they feel, how they feel, what makes
them upset, what's their opinion... Let them speak out about their
ideas, opinions, and feelings. That's important because by doing so
the child respects him/herself and his/her feelings and ideas. And
others should listen and pay attention to it. That's respect (field note,
Seminar 6, February, 1995).

Respecting differences by perceiving   and   understanding and allowing openness for children to express and show the importance of their own ideas, identity, and culture are understood as culturally congruent critical pedagogy (Hollings, King, & Hayman, 1994; Hyun, 1996; Ladson-Billings, 1992; Nieto, 1992). Ana's conceptualization of respect for the children's verbal expression of feelings and thoughts is a key component to her developing pedagogical sense of her DCAP.

However, Ana's voice made me think about how we can be sure that a teacher's expression of respect will be congruent with the child who comes from different family customs and culture, and who has a different perspective on expressions of respect. When Ana was asked about this matter, she responded:

> I have not thought about it actually. In fact we never learned about it. I mean how to approach it culturally differently/appropriately in terms of respect was never discussed in our teacher preparation ...Actually, in the matter of Anti-Bias Curriculum to multicultural education in my previous class, what I learned about the way of respecting diverse children was *listening* to their voices and helping them to *speak out* about their ideas and opinions...(field note, Seminar 6 February, 1995).

Some ethnic family cultures have developed more proficiency on nonverbal expressions of their feelings, ideas, and respect than other cultures. For example, the families of mainstream American culture in the United States employ more verbal expressions of respect than many families of other ethnic cultures. Many families of Native-American, African-American, Asian-American, and Hispanic-American practice nonverbal expressions and highly encourage nonverbal self-expressions of respect (McAdoo, 1993; Mindel, Habenstein & Wright, 1988).

What I learn from Ana's story is that teachers who want to adapt DCAP as culturally congruent critical pedagogy in their teaching profession need to know their students' diverse multiethnic perspectives (Banks, 1994a, b; Quintana, 1994) on expressions of respect which will help them appropriately interact with children from diverse perspectives.

Finally, problem solving is also an important concept for Ana's teachable moment-oriented DCAP lesson planning and implementation. She saw that DCAP helps young children learn problem solving skills for raising their self-esteem, which will lead them to be in control of their own lives:

> I have confidence that they can do it on their own if given the opportunity and if they have enough self-esteem to think that. And that's a big part of problem solving for my DCAP... If they are having a problem with somebody, they don't have to go tell the teacher, they can say, you know, Susan, I don't like when you talk to me like that and it hurts my feelings. That's problem solving, like they have to learn that they are in control of their own self and that what they say and do can change that (Ana's final interview, May 1995).

Ana's notion of helping young children's problem solving skills for her DCAP reflects the approach of Anti-Bias Curriculum and Education (Derman-Sparks, 1989). However, it is noteworthy that neither most typical teacher education materials used nor prospective teachers like Ana recognize that culture shapes the ways one approaches problem solving. Ana's expected idea of children's problem solving skills seemed more appropriate for single family ethnic cultural practice. Mainstream Americans' major characteristics of problem solving approaches are that they prefer to reason inductively, have a high value on self-reliance and autonomy, and encourage solving one's own problems and developing their own opinions (Stewart & Bennett, 1991).

However, according to cross-cultural psychologists and sociologists, ways of problem solving are diverse among diverse ethnic families. As examples, for the majority of African-American families, cooperation is a valuable approach to problem solving. Within the group cooperation many of them use internal cues for problem solving. For many Asian-American and Hispanic-American families, dependence on others for problem solving is acceptable because they also believe that it strengthens relationships among family members and other people (Becerra, 1988; Devore & London, 1993; Kain, 1993; Kitano, 1988; Locke, 1992; McAdoo, 1993; Min, 1988; Mindel, Habenstein, & Wright, 1988; Sanchez-Ayendez, 1988; Slonim, 1991; Staples, 1988; Stewart & Bennett, 1991; Szapocznik & Hernandez, 1988; Tran, 1988; Wilkinson, 1993; Williams, 1970; Wong, 1988). Thus, getting some support and help from teachers or other close peers may be appropriate to the child in a peer conflict. Teachers should support the child's personal approach to solving conflict or problems by understanding of the child's background, and should help the child to experience many different ways of problem solving for his/her future pluralistic social interactions.

Therefore, in order to properly learn and use culturally congruent DCAP, early childhood teachers like Ana need to realize, and teacher education contents should acknowledge the existence of multiple and multiethnic family perspectives on problem solving among children from diverse family backgrounds. Study of issues such as the way family culture shapes definitions of and approaches to problem solving may need to be included in the early childhood preservice teacher education curriculum to enable prospective teachers to recognize the impact of culture on such taken-for-granted skills as problem solving.

Although Ana realized that individual differences exist among all children in the classroom and tried to respect those differences in her DCAP teaching, this realization was not enough for Ana to acknowledge that there are diverse cultural approaches to problem solving. She was advocating a limited ethnic perspective-taking to enhance diverse young children's problem solving skills and individual self-expressions. Ana needed to know diverse family ethnic perspectives that affect each child's different ways of communicating respect and different ways of expressing self and solving problems. Clearly, in early childhood education teacher preparation programs for DCAP, more study is needed on the ways family culture shapes the children's and the teachers' thinking. In addition, a study of promoting prospective teachers' multiethnic family perspective-taking abilities in their future instruction for DCAP is needed.

Phenomena in Carrie's DCAP Sense Making

Carrie identified herself as a member of the "dominant" American culture from European descent:

> Where did my culture come from? I am of European descent--Irish, Italian, English, and German...My culture seems to be a rather prevalent one in society, so I feel no need to expect others to try to understand me--I am a member of the Dominant American culture. I don't feel that I have been at a disadvantage for being who I am (Carrie's autobiography, p.1, January 1995).

Carrie explained that her college coursework gave her an awareness regarding the need for change in the dominant society; that is, in attitudes toward gender roles and toward people of difference as well as in prevalent practices related to these perceptions. She believed that teachers have the power and the responsibility to act as agents of change in society:

> In our society, women are thought of as nurturing, sensitive, caring, and as mothers--which makes teaching a great career choice. If I had not taken some of the courses I had in college, I would be inclined to pass on to my students the kinds of injustices that seemed "natural" as I was growing up--for example: the White race is *the* dominant race, foreigners are freaks, men dominate women, there are men's jobs vs. women's jobs, the way things are is the way things should be--why change anything, etc. I've learned that teachers have the power and the responsibility to act as agents of change in society--we have a great deal of influence on young minds and that influence needs to be treated with the utmost respect (Carrie's autobiography p.2, January 1995).

One particular aspect of her teacher preparation that focused Carrie's interests on DCAP was her reading about culturally appropriate practice in early childhood education during her coursework. This reading was an important resource for Carrie's teacher preparation for DCAP:

> I've collected quite an extensive amount of literature, including children's books, on culturally appropriate practice through courses like ECE 451 (Foundation of ECE) and EDTHP 497A (Cultural Change) as well as through my own interest [in] the subject. Many of the articles I have were written by Louise Derman-Sparks, specifically applying culturally appropriate practice to early childhood education (Carrie's education that is multicultural self-assessment, pp. 1-2, January 1995).

Carrie felt that autobiographical self-awareness made her realize the importance of knowing one's own as well as others' cultures. She related this knowledge to equity in education:

> I have discovered for myself that the reason why the autobiographical self-awareness is so important to do is because, as a future teacher, I need to know how I feel about my culture and its importance as well as how much respect I have for cultures other than my own. I need to make myself aware of my prejudices before I bring them into the classroom... All students, regardless of ability, gender, race, ethnicity, or religion, have the right to the same education--same in the sense that they have equal opportunities to participate and learn. I feel that I have a better chance of teaching fairly after having reflected on my cultural background and its importance (Carrie's journal entry 3, January 1995).

From this early period in the semester, Carrie was one of the few students who showed her ability to construct self-knowledge and to understand how the dominant culture has shaped her thinking in a way that limits people's thinking and daily practices. Particularly, she was able to relate her future teaching to providing equal opportunities for learning.

She also showed me a strong commitment to DCAP during the entire field experience, as seen in both mid-term and final interviews:

> I want to make sure I have the right understanding of it [DCAP]...I want to make sure I am doing it [DCAP] in my lesson planning and teaching...(Carrie, mid-term conference interview, March 22, 1995).

> I figured out after I try and try and try and I was thinking this is stupid. And then I figured out--ooooh, each kid is different. Each kid had their own little family culture, they do what they do at home. They are different. And then I figured that out and then I decided how to go from there. How to reach them. And I have to admit I don't know that much about the kid's family background...You have to practice it... It just takes time and effort...I just want to have more practice doing what I'm doing...because for their sake, for the kids. It makes their learning experience better... And I paid more attention to the children, I think (Carrie's final interview, May 1995).

As Colton and Sparks-Langer (1992) indicate, the teacher of the future needs to be a self-directed person like Carrie who is intrinsically motivated to analyze a situation, set goals, plan and monitor actions, evaluate results, and reflect on her own DCAP teaching and learning.

As indicated by these quotes from her journals and interviews, Carrie expressed a strong commitment to DCAP from the beginning to the end of the semester. For this reason, Carrie became a participant in my study. The following section presents the ways in which Carrie made sense of DCAP over the course of the semester.

Field Placement

Carrie requested Green Preschool[11] in State College, for her placement because of its proximity to campus. The only reason she selected this school was that it would save her time since she said she was taking several other courses that kept her busy. She wanted to save some time and use her time more efficiently (field note, January 12, 1995).

At the time of Carrie's field placement, the classroom had fourteen preschoolers and two full-time teachers. One child was a special needs child, and four children were from a different ethnic background (Korean-American) than the other children. The cooperating teacher had thirteen years of teaching experience in early childhood and elementary education. However, this was her first experience as a cooperating teacher, and she was not familiar with culturally appropriate teaching and learning.

Even though Carrie wanted to have her teaching practice at this particular school, she was not happy with the classroom during the entire field experience. Her reason was that there was much less time given to child initiative free play, which Carrie believed is the most important aspect of a child's learning and development. During one of the field experience seminars Carrie said:

> I am learning about what is inappropriate for DCAP from my placement...I feel that I can learn from her [the cooperating teacher]. I've learned how important not to push the children based on the teacher's own project. There is not enough free play time for the children (field note, Seminar 6, February 16, 1995).

> There doesn't seem to be much modification on the part of the center to fit the needs of the children (Carrie's journal entry 8, p.1, March 1995).

> This whole semester I have focused on the importance of DCAP and each child having as equal an experience as possible... A lot of peers are in centers where it's easy to implement DCAP--where they can see this philosophy in practice. Unfortunately, I have not. I've had to struggle to get DCAP teaching experience... (Carrie's journal entry 12, April 1995).

Compared with Ana's placement, Carrie's school program and the cooperating teacher's practices could not support her teaching experience for learning developmental and cultural appropriateness. However, her self-motivated commitment toward DCAP made her constantly work on implementing DCAP in her field experience:

> I want to make sure I have the right understanding of it [DCAP]. And I don't want to blow it off or just, you know, brush it aside. I don't want to think that I have a good grip on it. I want to make sure I am doing it right. I guess that's the hardest part. I want to make sure I am doing it (Carrie, mid-term conference interview, March 22, 1995).

Because of Carrie's lack of meaningful observation and support for DCAP in her field placement, she relied heavily on her previous teacher preparation coursework, some readings, her personal self-awareness regarding culturally appropriate practice in teaching, and a self-motivated commitment to DCAP in order to make sense of what it means to be a DCAP teacher.

Carrie's Sense Making of DCAP

Carrie's initial definition of DCAP was that it is a philosophy of teaching that regards students' heritage, age, learning style, and prior experience, and how they can build upon it. But, after her lesson implementations, she redefined DCAP as providing an equal education:

> By implementing developmentally and culturally appropriate practice, as a teacher, you are giving each and every one of your students the opportunity to experience an equal education as equal as possible... (Carrie's journal entry 13, April 1995).

With Carrie's overall definition of DCAP as providing equal education, her notion of child initiative free play and the teacher's ongoing observation were the all encompassing means of how she made sense of DCAP lesson planning and implementation. Three of the most important components of Carrie's formulation of DCAP were (1) knowing individuality, (2) giving power to the child for learning, and (3) knowing and relating the child's family culture and past experiences to DCAP teaching and learning.

First, Carrie realized that knowing individual children very well is the major key to a DCAP lesson:

> Now I realized that it is absolutely necessary for a teacher to know his/her students very well. Otherwise it is not possible to create DCAP lessons. Each and every student needs to be considered individually in order to develop a truly DCAP lesson. (Carrie's lesson plan-1-self evaluation, February 1995)

Carrie frequently focused on each child's individual differences in their free play in her observations:

> ...each individual child in my classroom is different. Four are Korean children with limited English ability. One Korean child she has been here less than a month. I mean United States. Three of them are O.K. compared to her. I guess. I observed during the free play time they don't seemed to speak much compared to other English children, but they are doing great. One special needs child, he is an American. His attention span is terrible. You really have to work with him individually (field note - pre-conference with Carrie, March 1, 1995).

In recognizing individual differences, Carrie also recognized that many contemporary U.S. families are having, once in a while, somewhat unstable family structures or conditions for young children's development and learning, and that this instability affects the children's school lives:

> ...we [Carrie and her cooperating teacher] found out that he [a child in the class] is having a lot of problems at home. His favorite uncle moved out. I don't know, I thought maybe it was his mom's boyfriend, they just call him uncle, but it's not his dad. So I don't know. And all these things, he just got a new baby-sitter. I mean, he's one-on-one with you, he's very good. But he's the most disruptive in the classroom. Not because it's his fault. I think the classroom isn't

set up right for any kid. But he's the most disruptive...he hasn't been here much lately. He wasn't there at all this week...We see these kids all the time in these days, in very early childhood classrooms (Carrie's final interview, May 1995).

While Carrie could recognize the importance of focusing on individual differences, she had a difficulty in translating her observations of differences to her teaching. For example, during one pre-conference observation, I asked Carrie:

"How would you like to help the children with a limited English speaking and understanding? And how about the child who seems to need special attention from the teacher during the lesson?"
Carrie said, "I don't know. I have no idea. Johnny, the one who has a short attention span, I have to just ignore him sometimes if I want to finish the lesson...Tomorrow when you come, see them [the children with limited English proficiency] and give them some ideas" (field note: pre-conference with Carrie, March 1, 1995).

Following this comment, I tried to further facilitate Carrie's mental planning for her diverse teaching by offering some instructional ideas:

"Would you like to try to incorporate some of their home language for the lesson?"
Carrie's face just went blank. She did not say anything regarding this suggestion. Just stared at me (I was thinking, she may not think that it is necessary for her lesson preparation (field note: pre-conference with Carrie, March 1, 1995).

Culturally congruent critical pedagogy for young children employs the children's personal experience, family culture, and diverse languages as important sources of learning and teaching (Nieto, 1992). Even though the teacher does not speak the other language, she/he can invite the children to incorporate their own home language into the experience to make the children's learning personally meaningful and culturally relevant (as Ana and her cooperating teacher did), and welcome the children's family members and parents to join the activity.

Realizing the existence of individual differences and that they are not only limited to a child's ethnic or racial background but also to the child's personal developmental maturity, previous experience, and unique family culture, practices, and current circumstance are fundamental to a teacher's conceptualization of DCAP. Yet, I learn from Carrie that recognition of individual differences may not necessarily translate into a teacher's practice. Carrie was able to recognize and consider individual children's differences in their learning which could be derived from the child's physical/mental uniqueness, nationality, or different home language and cultures. She also was able to interpret each child's current family situation or structure that affects the young child's development, learning and school life. However, she had a limit expanding her awareness to develop diverse teaching approaches, such as incorporating the learner's native language into the learning experience--as in Ana's case--or trying to find a way to help the child who seemed to need a personal meaningful learning approach, so that she could bring an equal learning experience to them as she defined DCAP.

This limitation may be due to her teacher preparation program. Despite Carrie's view of considering individuality in the lesson as an important aspect of DCAP, Carrie, like Ana, had difficulty making sense of the way she was taught to plan lessons during her teacher preparation program in relation to her developing notions of DCAP:

> Child-initiated free play oriented lesson would be appropriate for DCAP because it's what they've chosen to do themselves. Each child is different--each brings different background and experience to the learning environment--that it would be impossible to create a universally DCAP lesson. It was somewhat of a new experience planning for DCAP in my lesson. That may sound strange, but in the past (my social studies methods class for example) the lesson plans I've created were rather generic. They were developed for a

> hypothetical class in which DCAP had no place (Carrie's journal entry
> 8, p.2, April 1995).

Similar to Ana, Carrie believes that it is impossible to create generic lesson plans for DCAP because each child is different and makes sense of learning differently. It may be that Carrie was unable to translate her recognition and knowledge of individual differences into her instruction because of a limited perception of what it means to plan a lesson. Once again, this incident points to the need for teacher preparation programs to be flexible in requirements for lesson planning, as well as to present various models and different perspectives on lesson planning in early childhood education.

Second, Carrie determined that DCAP gave power to the children by encouraging them to think and verbally express their ideas. She found particular value for children to learn problem solving based on their perspectives:

> In my DCAP... I am thinking...how to give power to the child as
> opposed to the teacher having all the power. Asking the child an open-
> ended question gives the child power and encourages him/her to think
> or at least to verbally express his/her mental strategies. Even if the
> child's logic is not all that "logical" yet, the point is that the child is
> learning to solve problems based on his/her own perspective (Carrie's
> journal entry 5, February 1995).

According to Carrie, asking divergent questions brings a developmentally and culturally congruent learning and teaching experience to children. In one lesson she asked the following questions and then reflected on these questions as creating a DCAP lesson for the children:

> Do you remember when you did the morning art activity about
> making a lion? How was your lion's face? Was it smiling? or sad?
> ...Do you remember when your mother or father took you to get a
> haircut? What did you see there? What was your feeling when you
> were there? (Field note, Carrie's lesson observation, March 2, 1995).

> I was able to incorporate their comments and questions into the lesson
> successfully. Actually, now that I think about it, it was those questions
> and comments that made the lesson developmentally and culturally
> appropriate. I felt that I know enough about the students' lives to be
> able to relate what's been going on with them in their lives to the
> story, poem, and discussion (Carrie's lesson plan-1-self evaluation,
> February 1995).

Carrie's notion of giving power to the child for their learning often included divergent questioning. It made sense to her that by accepting children's questions and comments, responding to them, and providing divergent questions related to their comments, the individual child could relate his/her prior knowledge, experience, and family background to the lesson and the learning experiences.

In summary, in order to help children create their own developmentally and culturally appropriate learning experience, Carrie felt that the teacher's role is to pose divergent questions. This practice was central to Carrie's notion of DCAP. Generally, this notion sounds acceptable and appropriate, but there is a critical concern. In many cases Carrie's divergent questions were not inherently culturally congruent. For example, the families of some children in Carrie's class do their hair cutting at their home as a family routine. What Carrie did not know is that, in particular, most of the children from diverse family backgrounds in Carrie's school do their hair cutting at home, especially when the children are a young age of up to 3 or 4. Therefore, the question Carrie posed during her lesson, "Do you remember when your mother or father took you to get a haircut? What did you see there? What was your feeling when you were there?" might not be culturally congruent for all of the children. Carrie never realized her question might not be developmentally and culturally congruent for all learners. A developmentally and culturally appropriate questioning style might be: "How do you get a haircut?" "Who does it for you?" "How does the person take care of your hair when the person fixes your hair?" "How do you feel about it?" "How do you express your feelings of getting a haircut when the person is doing it for you?" The key in divergent questioning style is to bring the question that leads the individual young children to construct their own answers that are developmentally and culturally congruent for them.

To pose a developmentally and culturally congruent divergent question, a teacher must have a good knowledge or understanding of each child's personal mental and physical maturity, background, previous experiences, and family ethnic culture. Otherwise, the teacher's divergent question may not fit each child's development and culture. A danger occurs when a teacher relies on simplistic open-ended questioning formulated from the teacher's perspective as opposed to considering the child's perspectives when formulating questions.

Lastly, as time passed during the field experience, Carrie realized that a key component of DCAP is the teacher's respect for each child's unique family culture and practices, and reflection of this respect in each teacher-child interaction.

> I want to meet the parents. I want to be there when the parents come in...You can kind of know what to expect when you meet the parents...And just the way they interact with the kids helps you to know what the kids expect out of interaction with adults. If they're very touchy feely, the kids would be more clingy than if, or be more likely to, than if the parents don't touch, you know, they don't pat them on the head or hug before they say good-bye. Then the kids probably wouldn't be that prone to physical contact. Maybe they would. Maybe that would make them want it more. You can figure that out as you go. That is important for me to know (Carrie's final interview, May 1995).

This type of sense making by Carrie seemed quite appropriate for DCAP. It would be helpful if a DCAP teacher preparation model provided a pedagogical knowledge using field-based case studies in cross-cultural/or multiethnic family characteristics which directly affect diverse individual young children's learning and development.

Implications and Conclusion

The theoretical framework of social phenomenology and the conceptual framework of DCAP teacher preparation that I used in this study allowed me to see my participants' construction of DCAP sense making and guided me to construct some suggestions for promoting early childhood teacher preparation. In this section I present and discuss assertions that have emerged from a collective examination of Ana and Carrie's individual stories, along with possible implications and suggestions for further research.

Assertion 1: Creating an equal learning experience for all individual children is an important component of DCAP. Yet the prospective teachers' recognition of the importance of individuality in DCAP may be constrained by a limited ethnic family perspective on learning and teaching.

Even though Ana and Carrie's definition of DCAP varied to some degree, there was one common aspect in their definition. They agree that providing an equal learning experience for all individual children is an important component of DCAP.

Much has been written from a multicultural education perspective about what an equal learning experience should mean in schools as it relates to race, gender, culture, language, and disability (Sleeter & Grant, 1994). Yet, in this study the two participants conceptually tried to relate equal learning experience to individuality. Instead of looking at children based on a group identity such as race or gender as presented in Sleeter and Grant (1994), discovering each child's unique individuality was an important aspect of the way the prospective teachers made sense of DCAP in this study.

By observing diverse children in the classroom, these two participants discovered young children's individual differences in their learning. They felt that addressing and respecting individual differences in their DCAP lesson planning and implementation would bring an equal learning experience to their students. However, focusing on individuality is not sufficient to provide an equal learning experience. The classroom conditions and the DCAP teachers' mind-set should be flexible and divergent. Teachers need to be multilingual, multiperspective, and multidimensional in their focus (Sizemore, 1979; Sleeter & Grant, 1994). In this aspect, Carrie and Ana's implementation of DCAP for providing equal learning experience was limited. While Ana and Carrie focused on the individuality of each child in their classroom, a limited ethnic approach and understanding of such concepts as respect, problem solving, and divergent questioning dominated their practice.

Hence, more discussion is needed in teacher education programs on culture and the ways in which culture shapes not only the child's learning and development but also the teachers' thinking. One component of discussion of culture that is often absent in teacher education programs is family ethnicity. Both Carrie and Ana related heavily on family culture in discovering the individual identity of each child in their classes:

> If it's their family life or if it's how they approach situations differently or whatever it is you have to always be aware of it and be ready to help them develop their own self-identity and the individuality (Ana's mid-term interview, March 1995).

> I want to meet the parents. I want to be there when the parents come in. You can kind of know what to expect when you meet the parents. And just the way they interact with the kids helps you to know what the kids expect out of interaction with adults. If they're very touchy feely, the kids would be more clingy than if, or be more likely to [hug], than if the parents don't touch, you know, they don't pat them on the head or hug [them] before they say good-bye. Then the kids probably wouldn't be that prone to physical contact. Maybe they would. Maybe that would make them want it more. You can figure that out as you go. That is important for me to know for my DCAP (Carrie's final interview, May 1995).

Yet, limited knowledge of family ethnicity contributed to their limited understanding of how family ethnicity shapes one's understanding of such concepts as respect and problem solving. According to Reiff and Cannella (1990) and the two participants in this study, prospective early childhood teachers feel the least confident about their familiarity with childrearing practices and the history of culturally diverse families. Early childhood teachers who work with diverse ethnic children and families will be far more effective if they have accurate information about their students' unique family cultures and ethnic backgrounds. If knowledge about family ethnicity is incorporated within children's family experience and background, teachers will have richer resources with which to help the children learn (McAdoo, 1993). As Ana and Carrie said, prospective teachers need to learn more about other ethnic family characteristics and the changing dynamics in their social contexts in order to properly facilitate diverse children's development and earning.

Hence, in teaching for DCAP, teacher preparation programs need to have a component that provides a fundamental learning opportunity for prospective teachers to know what family ethnicity is and what makes each family unique, what are the dynamics of changing family ethnic cultures, how that particular ethnicity affects young children's play, learning, and development, and why it is important to know as a early childhood DCAP teacher. More research and development is needed in this area.

Assertion 2: The writing of structured lesson plans, common in teacher education programs, may constrain the way prospective teachers make sense of and implement DCAP.

Writing a generic lesson plan based on lesson objectives, rationale, transition/motivation, behavior expectation, major procedures, lesson sequences, closure, transition, and so on, is common practice in teacher preparation (i.e., Walsh, 1980; Wortham, 1998). However, Ana and Carrie mentioned frequently that the idea of standard or generic written lesson planning, which they had learned from their previous teacher education courses, seemed inappropriate for DCAP because each child's learning style and their sense making of the learning is diverse. The generic lesson planning experienced in their teacher education coursework did not give these preservice teachers an awareness of or practice in planning for diverse young children's individuality in their teaching.

These prospective teachers discovered the inconsistency between their teacher preparation program's notion of lesson planning and their developing sense of DCAP during their lesson implementation. As Carrie and Ana implemented their lesson plans, they engaged in ongoing self-monitored reflection to see whether their prepared lessons were developmentally and culturally appropriate to the child, or whether they needed to make changes during the lesson itself. They also had to consider what changes in their plans might be appropriate for the individual children in their class during the lesson. During this process, they often realized that despite the preparation of a formal lesson plan, they had no idea what would be appropriate for the reality of the individual children in their class.

This phenomenon led me to inquire as to how early childhood teacher preparation for DCAP can help prospective teachers have a better perception of learning about developing formal lesson planning and use of it with teacher's instructional reflection and flexible approaches for early childhood education. Whenever prospective teachers learn about developing lesson plans in their teacher preparation period, they need to have a real practical picture of target children for the lesson planning. One promising way to accomplish this on a college campus may be the use of some reality-based cases (Dana & Floyd, 1993; Kowalski, Weaver, & Henderson, 1990; Locke, 1992; Merseth, 1991 & 1992; Shulman, 1992) and heavily rely on field-based observation of children's play and interactive participation approaches.

Cases focusing on: cross-cultural child development and learning; cross-cultural children's play; diversified individual needs among learners; multiethnic parents' educational practices and expectations toward the school and early childhood teachers may provide a context for which prospective teachers can discuss not only the "how to teach" or "what to teach" of lesson planning, but also the issues inherent in planning interactions--of what they want to learn and how they want to explore it--with diverse individual children.

Most importantly, DCAP lesson planning in conjunction with reality-based case study should incorporate several self-critical questions such as:

> *(1) In what sense is this activity/lesson age appropriate?*
> *(2) In what ways can my lesson content/context/procedures support diverse individual children's learning and developmental characteristics?*
> *(3) In what ways does my DCAP lesson properly respond to each individual child's meaningful learning experience so that everybody has an equal and culturally congruent learning experience?*
> *(4) How can I incorporate children's home language in my daily practice to support home language preservation?*
> *(5) How can I incorporate children's family cultures as teaching and learning resources?*

These inquiries should always be presented by instructors when prospective teachers learn about lesson plan in their early childhood teacher preparation for DCAP.

Lessons based on child's play-based teachable moments should also be emphasized, especially when prospective teachers are in a field experience. In order for them to develop a critical pedagogy for DCAP in early childhood education, field supervisors need to encourage student teachers' keen observation in child initiative free play and classroom conditions such as curriculum and classroom culture. Supervisors should suggest that they think about a series of critical inquiries in conjunction with teachable moment oriented DCAP lesson planning and implementation. For example:

What have you discovered about the classroom and the children?
What was your discovery of each individual child's characteristics of learning and development?
What makes you think that each individual has his or her own characteristics of learning and development?
What makes you think that the individual child's characteristics bring diversity into the classroom?

What type of diversity exists in child-initiate free play?
In what ways can child initiative free play become a teachable moment, so that you can use it as a culturally and developmentally congruent DCAP play-based learning experiences for the child?

In what ways did the classroom environment and the teachers support each child's unique needs for his/her own learning and development? How was the classroom culture expressed?

Was the classroom culture fair to all children so that they could continuously develop positive self-esteem, and create their own culturally congruent child-initiative free play?
If it is a less congruent classroom condition for all individual children, what led you to think in that way?
What alternative ways would you like to try for your own DCAP teaching based on your observation of child initiative free play?

In order to help early childhood prospective teachers to use DCAP as a critical pedagogy, seeking flexible and divergent ways to learn lesson planning will be more appropriate than following a standard lesson plan format. Reality based case study for lesson planning and teachable moment oriented lessons along with having an actual target child in prospective teachers' mind will be the key in learning about planning for DCAP teaching. Additional research and development need to be completed on the teaching of divergent ways of lesson planning and its relationship to DCAP early childhood teacher preparation.

New Perspectives on DCAP Teacher Preparation

This study brought a new perspective in the theoretically oriented early childhood teacher preparation for DCAP. It was developed in regard to the need for a teacher preparation procedure that can help prospective teachers to develop diverse multiethnic family perspective-taking abilities into their divergent lesson planning and implementation, which are appropriate to early childhood.

The original theory of teacher preparation for DCAP and other related literatures advocated that prospective teachers need to know family ethnicity as a knowledge base, at least, to make their future teaching that is multicultural. However, until this study began, there was not enough evidence from prospective teachers in the field to support that need. The results of this study clearly present the need to study family ethnicities that directly affect children's development, learning, and problem solving skills.

Through this study I now begin to see the needs and ways of studying family ethnicity as a critical component in teacher preparation. Prospective teachers need to know United States diverse families ethnic practices and the contemporary changing dynamics within the families, all of which form young individual children's developmental characteristics and their unique understanding of their own learning. Teacher educators need to search for a meaningful way to introduce multiple perspectives on diverse family ethnicities that affect young children's learning and development. Simultaneously, teacher educators need to help prospective teachers develop multiple perspective-taking abilities in their instructional planning so that it becomes more teachable-moment oriented, and negotiable thus responds to the true nature of young children's learning and early childhood education.

Conclusion

United States educational society is less certain today that there is a "one best" set of cultural beliefs and educational practices. A "one best" approach *could not, cannot*, and *will not* achieve an equal education for all (Bowman, 1994; Delpit, 1995; Jipson, 1991).

Early childhood teacher educators, prospective teachers, and practitioners must question whether the traditional definition of developmentally appropriate practice (DAP) is facilitating an equal education for *all* children that would support the power of multiple perspectives in diverse young children's culturally congruent learning and development. If we see DAP as the one best approach for early childhood education we can all easily become product oriented practitioners who may be less sensitive to the multidirectional processes of young children's developmental changes and learning styles as derived from their own ethnic family cultures. Realizing the multiple phenomena of diverse young children's developmental changes and growth requires that teachers be *process oriented reflective professionals* as DCAP practitioners.

Bowman's (1992, 1994) insight on preparing teachers for culturally appropriate practice inspired me to realize the need of teacher preparation for both developmentally and culturally appropriate practice in early childhood education. My model of early childhood teacher preparation for developmentally and culturally appropriate practice was developed for helping prospective teachers develop a process oriented pedagogical sense of multiple perspectives in their teaching. This qualitative study was conducted in order to explore who prospective teachers are and what these teachers think and understand about developmentally and culturally appropriate practice when they are in a clinical teaching experience. The results of this study helped to clearly develop the theoretical model for DCAP into a more practical mode that can be implemented in early childhood teacher education. It is hoped that the results of this study and this book will serve as a point of departure for continued dialogue, discussion, and debate regarding DCAP and its place in the preparation of early childhood teachers.

Notes

1. Pseudonym used in this text.

2. Multiple/multiethnic perspective-taking is an individual's cognitive capacity to construct his/her understanding of self, other, and social phenomena through first-, second-, and third-person perspective-taking. The ability to step out of one's own cultural paradigm and assume that the existence of multiple realities inevitably leads to divergence in all human endeavor is the ultimate form of multiple/multiethnic perspective-taking. Multiple/multiethnic perspectives represent diverse peoples' diverse sense making of living, problem solving, learning, and so on, derived from not only their intra-ethnic (each family's ethnic and cultural formation that is unique to their own "group" ethnic cultures) phenomena but also their inter-ethnic (ethnic "group" culture that interacts with each individual family culture) relations (Hyun & Marshall, 1997).

3. Pseudonyms have been used in this study report.

4. For previous work that has been done in the theory of developing multiple and multiethnic perspective-taking abilities by Hyun and Marshall (1997). This section in Chapter 3 is a modified section of this article with permission from the other author.

5. Interpersonal Negotiation Strategies (INS) developed by Selman and Schultz (1990) illustrate the dependent relations between a person's social perspective developmental level and his or her interpersonal orientation.

    The INS model assumes that 1) coordination of social perspectives is intrinsic to the process of balancing personal and interpersonal needs in ongoing relationships, and that 2) mature negotiation is based on the increasing ability to coordinate (i.e., differentiate and integrate) the perspectives of self and other. Four developmental levels of interpersonal negotiation reflect different levels of sophistication in perspective coordination; Within the INS model, strategies classified as Level 0 are primitive--physical and impulsive, usually driven by "out of control" feelings like rage or panic. Here, people exhibit a lack of reflection on or coordination of the perspectives of self and other in the consideration of a particular social problem.

Level 1 strategies reflect a "one-way" perspective. At this level, although it is recognized that the perspectives of self and other may differ in the particular situation and that the parties must interact to resolve the conflict, strategies are not coordinated based on the simultaneous consideration of the two perspectives. These often power-oriented negotiations include one-way commands and orders or, conversely, simple and unchallenging accommodations (giving in) to the perceived needs and demands of the other person. This type of interpersonal negotiation strategy may lead people to certain limits in their social contexts.

Strategies at Level 2 are psychologically based, reciprocal exchanges which require the perspectives of both self and other in order to reflect upon the negotiation from a second-person perspective. At this level, both self and other are planful and self-reflective; the thoughts, feelings, and actions of each influence those of the other. Level 2 strategies include psychological trades and exchanges, verbal persuasion or deference, convincing others, making deals, and other forms of self-interested cooperation. At this level, the self may defer to the other but not show respect totally.

Collaborative (Level 3) strategies represent a consideration of the need for an *integration* of the interests of self and other. Thus, the negotiation is viewed from a third-person perspective. These strategies involve compromise, dialogue, process analysis, and the development of a shared goal of mutual understanding. Here, an understanding exists that concern for the relationship's continuity over time is a necessary consideration for the adequate, fair, and optimal solution of any immediate problem.

Although all these components are intertwined in conduct, it is useful to explore them separately while remaining cautious about *not* reducing complex social conflicts to four deceptively simplistic levels of interpersonal negotiation. Moreover, the four component levels are not a traditional hierarchical scoring system but rather a clinical reference guide for a negotiation strategy or series of strategies. With developmental maturity, according to Selman and Schultz, one's interpersonal orientation shifts toward collaborative actions which synthesize differentiated conceptions and perceptions of self and other, and represent a mixture of accommodation and assertion, entailing simultaneous attempts to change self and other (Hyun & Marshall, 1997).

6. This chapter is modified version of Hyun & Marshall, "Inquiry-Oriented Reflective Supervision for Developmentally and Culturally Appropriate Practice," *Journal of Curriculum and Supervision,* Winter 1996. 11, 1:127-144. Reprinted with permission of the association for Supervision and Curriculum Development. Copyright © 1996 by ASCD. All rights reserved.

7. These questions are adapted and modified from the works of Grant (1981), Renwick (1974), and Hyun & Marshall (1996). Additional revision were made in 1997 for this text.

8. Pseudonyms have been used in the study.

9. Pseudonyms have been used in the study.

10. Actual name of the school site was not used in the study.

11. Actual name of the school site was not used in the study.

References

Acheson, K. A., & Gall, M. D. (1992). *Techniques in the clinical supervision of teachers: Preservice and inservice applications.* White Plains, NY: Longman.

Acheson, K. A., Anderson, R., & Krajewski, R. (1980). *Clinical supervision of teachers: Preservice and inservice applications.* White Plains, NY: Longman.

Au, K. (1993). *Literacy instruction in multicultural settings.* Orlando, FL: Holt, Rinehart & Winston.

Au, K., & Kawakami, A. (1985). Research currents: Talk story and learning to read. *Language Arts, 62* (4), 406-411.

Ayers, W. (1989). *The good preschool teacher: Six teachers reflect on their lives.* New York: Teachers College Press.

Baker, G. C. (1994). *Planning and organizing for multicultural instruction.* New York: Addison-Wesley.

Banks, J. (1994a). *Multiethnic education: Theory and practice.* Boston: Allyn & Bacon.

Banks, J. (1994b). *An introduction to multicultural education.* Boston: Allyn & Bacon.

Becerra, R. M. (1988). The Mexican American family. In C. H. Mindel, R. W. Habenstein, & R. Wright. (Eds.), *Ethnic families in America: Patterns and variations* (3rd ed.). Englewood Cliffs, NJ: Prentice-Hall.

Berk, L. E. (1994). *Child development*. Needham Heights, MA: Allyn & Bacon.

Berliner, D. C. (1986). In pursuit of the expert pedagogue. *Educational Researcher, 15* (7), 5-13.

Bloch, M., Adler, S. (1994). African children's play and the emergence of the sexual division of labor. In J. Roopnarine, J. Johnson, & F. Hooper (Eds.), *Children's play in diverse cultures* (pp. 148-178). Albany, NY: SUNY Press.

Bogdan, R. C., & Bicklen, S. K. (1992). *Qualitative research for education*. Boston: Allyn & Bacon.

Bowers, C. A., & Flinders, A. J. (1991). *Culturally responsive teaching and supervision*. New York: Teachers College Press.

Bowman, B. (1994). Thoughts on educating teachers. In S. G. Goffin & D. E. Day (Eds.). *New perspectives in early childhood teacher education: Bringing practitioners into the debate* (pp. 210-214). New York: Teachers College Press.

Bowman, B. (1992). Reaching potentials of minority children through developmentally and culturally appropriate program. In S. Bredekamp, & T. Rosegrant (Eds.). *Reaching potentials: Appropriate curriculum and assessment for young children* (pp. 128-138). Washington, DC: National Association for the Education of Young Children.

Bowman, B. (1989). *Self-reflection as an element of professionalism*. New York: Teachers College Record, 90, 444-451.

Bredekamp, S. (Ed.). (1987). *Developmentally appropriate practice in early childhood programs serving children from birth through age 8*. (Rev. ed.). Washington, DC: National Association for the Education of Young Children.

Bredekamp, S., & Copple, C. (Eds.). (1997). *Developmentally appropriate practice in early childhood programs (revised edition)*. Washington, DC: National Association for the Education of Young Children.

Bredekamp, S., & Rosegrant, T. (Eds.). (1992). *Reaching potentials: Appropriate curriculum and assessment for young children*. Washington, DC: National Association for the Education of Young Children.

Brenner, J., & Mueller, E. (1982). Shared meaning in boy toddlers' peer relations. *Child Development, 53*, 380-381.

Cannella, C., & Reiff, J. (1994). Preparing teachers for cultural diversity: Constructivistic orientations. *Action in Teacher Education, 16* (3), 37-45.

Chandler, M. J. (1982). Social cognition and social structure. In F. C. Serafica (Ed.), *Social cognitive development in context* (pp. 222-239). New York: Guilford.

Colton, A. B., & Sparks-Langer, G. (1993). A conceptual framework to guide the development of teacher reflection and decision making. *Journal of Teacher Education, 44* (1), 45-54.

Colton, A. B., & Sparks-Langer, G. (1992). Restructuring student teaching experiences. In C.D. Glickman (Ed.), *Supervision in transition: 1992 Yearbook of the Association for Supervision and Curriculum Development* (pp. 155-168). Alexandria, VA: Association for Supervision and Curriculum Development.

Dana, N. F. (1993). Supervising teachers of young children: Developmentally appropriate educational practices and beyond. *Pennsylvania Educational Leadership, 12* (2), 7-12.

Dana, N. F. (1992, February). *Towards preparing the monocultural teacher for the multicultural classroom*. Paper presented at the annual meeting of the Association of Teacher Educators, Orlando, FL.

Dana, N. F., & Floyd, D.M. (1993, February). *Preparing preservice teachers for the multicultural classroom: A report on the case study approach.* Paper presented at the annual meeting of the Association of Teacher Educators Conference, Los Angeles, CA.

Delpit, L. D. (1995). *Other people's children: Cultural conflict in the classroom.* New York: The New.

Delpit, L. D. (1988). The silenced dialogue: Power and pedagogy in educating other people's children. *Harvard Educational Review, 58* (3), 280-287.

Derman-Sparks, L. (1992). Reaching potentials through antibias multicultural curriculum. In S. Bredekamp, & T. Rosegrant (Eds.), *Reaching potentials: Appropriate curriculum and assessment for young children* (pp. 114-127). Washington, DC: National Association for the Education of Young Children.

Derman-Sparks, L., & the A.B.C. Task Force. (1989). *Anti-bias curriculum: Tools for empowering young children.* Washington, DC: National Association for the Education of Young Children.

Devore, W., & London, H. (1993). Ethnic sensitivity for practitioners. In H.P. McAdoo (ed.) *Family ethnicity strength in diversity.* Newbury Park, CA: SAGE.

Eisenberg, N., & Miller, P.A. (1987). The relation of empathy to prosocial and related behaviors. *Psychological Bulletin, 101* (1), 91-119.

Erikson, E. H. (1963). *Childhood and society.* NY: Norton.

Erickson, F., & Mohatt, G. (1982). Cultural organization and participation structures in two classrooms of Indian studies. In G. Spindler (Ed.), *Doing the ethnography of schooling* (pp. 132-174). Orlando, FL: Holt, Rinehart & Winston.

Fuller, M. (1992). Teacher education programs and increasing minority school populations: An educational mismatch? In C. Grant (Ed.), *Research and multicultural education: From the margins to the mainstream* (pp. 184-200). Bristol, PA: Falmer.

Fuller, F., & Bowen, O. (1975). Becoming a teacher. In K. Ryan (Ed.), *Teacher education*. Seventy-fourth Yearbook of the National Society for the Study of Education, Part III (pp. 25-52). Chicago: University of Chicago Press.

Gardner, H. (1983). *Frames of mind: The theory of multiple intelligences*. New York: Basic Books.

Gestwicki, C. (1995). *Developmentally appropriate practice: Curriculum and development in early childhood education*. Albany, NY: Delmer.

Gipe, J. P., & Richards, J. C. (1992). Reflective thinking and growth in novices' teaching abilities. *Journal of Educational Research, 86* (1), 52-57.

Giroux, H. A., & Simon, R. (1989). Schooling, popular culture, and a pedagogy of possibility. *Journal of Education, 170* (1), 9-26.

Glickman, C. D. (1990). *Supervision of instruction: A developmental approach* (2nd ed.). Boston: Allyn & Bacon.

Goldhammer, R., Anderson, R., & Krajewski, R. (1980). *Clinical supervision*. New York: Holt, Rinehart & Winston.

Goldsberry, J. (1986). Is clinical supervision practical? In W. J. Smyth (Ed.), *Learning about teaching through clinical supervision* (137-153). London: Croom Helm.

Goodlad, J. (1990). *Teachers for our nation's schools*. San Francisco, CA: Jossey Bass.

Gore, J. (1987). Reflecting on reflective teaching. *Journal of Teacher*

Education, *38* (2), 33-39.

Grant, C. A. (1992). (Ed.). *Research and multicultural education: From the margins to the mainstream*. Bristol, PA: Falmer.

Grant, C. A. (1981). Education that is multicultural and teacher preparation: An examination from the perspectives of preservice students. *Journal of Education Research*, *75* (2), 95-101.

Grant, C. A., & Zeichner, K. M. (1984). On becoming a reflective teacher. In C.A. Grant (Ed.), *Preparing for reflective teaching* (pp. 1-18). Boston: Allyn and Bacon.

Gutman, A. (1987). *Democratic education*. Princeton, NJ: Princeton University Press.

Henderson, J. (1988). A curriculum response to the knowledge base reform movement. *Journal of Teacher Education*, *39*, 13-17.

Hinchey, P. (1994). Introducing diversity: We don't have to wait for a program. *Action in Teacher Education*, *16* (3), 28-36.

Hollins, E., King, J., & Hayman, W. (1994). (Eds.). *Teaching diverse populations: Formulating a knowledge base*. New York: SUNY Press.

Holstein, J., Gubrium, J. (1994). Phenomenology, ethnomethodology, and interpretive practice. In N. Denzin, & Y. Lincoln (Eds.), *Handbook of qualitative research* (pp. 262-272). Newbury Park, CA: SAGE.

Howes, C. (1988). Peer interaction of young children. *Monographs of the Society for Research in Child Development*, 53 (Serial No. 17).

Howes, C. (1980). Peer play scale as an index of complexity of peer interaction. *Developmental Psychology*, *16*, 371-372.

Howes, C., & Matheson, C. C. (1992). Sequences in the development of competent play with peers; Social and social pretend play. *Developmental Psychology, 28*, 961-974.

Howes, C., Unger, O., & Seidner, L. B. (1989). Social pretend play in toddlers: Parallels with social play and with solitary pretend play. *Child Development, 60*, 77-84.

Huberman, M. (1991). Can cultural awareness be taught in teacher education programs? *Teaching Education, 4* (1), 25-31.

Hughes, F. (1995). *Children, play and development*. Needham Heights, MA: Allyn and Bacon.

Hyman, R., & Rosoff, B. (1988). Matching learning styles and teaching styles: The jug and what's in it. *Theory into Practice, 23* (1), 35-43.

Hyun, E. (1997). *Self-examination of one's own ethnicity in the context of teacher preparation for a pluralistic society*. Paper presented at the 1997 Annual Conference of American Educational Research Association (AERA).

Hyun, E. (1996). New directions early childhood teacher preparation: Developmentally and culturally appropriate practice (DCAP). *Journal of Early Childhood Teacher Education, 17* (3), 7-19.

Hyun, E. (1995). *Preservice teachers' sense making of developmentally and culturally appropriate practice (DCAP) in early childhood education*. Doctoral dissertation, The Pennsylvania State University, PA.

Hyun, E., & Dana, F. (In press). Bringing developmentally and culturally appropriate practice in early childhood teacher education. *Journal of Early Childhood Teacher Education*.

Hyun, E., Marshall, J. D. (1997). Theory of multiple/multiethnic perspective-taking ability for teachers' developmentally and culturally appropriate practice (DCAP). *Journal of Research in Childhood Education, 11* (2), 188-198.

Jipson, J. (1991). Developmentally appropriate practice: Culture, curriculum, connections. *Early Education and Development, 2* (2), 120-136.

Johnson, J. E., Christie, J. F., & Yawkey, T. D. (1987). *Play and early childhood development*. Glenview, IL: Scott, Foresman and Company.

Jordan, C. (1985). Translating culture: From ethnographic information to educational program. *Enthnopology and Education Quarterly, 16* (2), 105-123.

Kagan, D. M. (1989). The heuristic value of regarding classroom instruction as an aesthetic medium. *Educational Researcher, 18* (6), 11-18.

Kain, E. L. (1993). Race, mortality, and families. In H. P. McAdoo (ed.) *Family ethnicity strength in diversity*. Newbury Park, CA: SAGE.

Kelly, M., & Surbeck, E. (1991). *Restructuring early childhood education*. Bloomington, IN: Phi Delta Kappa Education Foundation.

Kennedy, M. (1990). *NCRTL special report: An agenda for research on teacher learning*. East Lansing, MI: National Center for Research on Teacher Learning.

Kilbourn, B. (1982). Linda: A case study in clinical supervision. *Canada Journal of Education, 7* (3), 1-24.

Killion, J., & Todnem, G. (1991). A process for personal theory building. *Educational leadership, 48* (6), 14-16.

Kincheloe, J. (1993). *Toward a critical politics of teacher thinking: Mapping the postmodern.* Westport, CT: Bergin & Garvey.

Kitano, H. H. L. (1988). The Japanese American family. In C. H. Mindel, R. W. Habenstein, & R. Wright. (Eds.), *Ethnic families in America: Patterns and variations.* Englewood Cliffs, NJ: Prentice-Hall.

Kowalski, T., Weaver, R. A., & Henderson, K. (1990). *Case studies on teaching.* New York: Longman.

Kumabe, K. T., Nishida, C., & Hepworth, D.H. (1985). *Bridging ethnocultural diversity in social work and health.* Honolulu: University of Hawaii, School of Social Work.

Ladson-Billings, G. (1994). Who will teach our children? Preparing teachers to successfully teach African American students. In E. Hollins, J. King, & W. Hayman (Eds.), *Teaching diverse populations: Formulating a knowledge base* (pp. 231-245). New York: SUNY Press.

Ladson-Billings, G. (1992). Culturally relevant teaching: The key to making multicultural education work. In C. Grant (Ed.), *Research and multicultural education: From the margins to the mainstream* (pp. 106-121). Bristol, PA: Falmer.

Larke, P., Wiseman, D., & Bradley, C. (1990). *The minority mentorship program: Educating teachers for diverse classrooms'. Multicultural Teacher Education Research in the 1990s conference proceedings,* (pp. 70-80), College Station, TX.

Lasley, T. J. (1992). Promoting teacher reflection. *Journal of Staff Development, 13* (1), 24-29.

LeCompte, M., & Preissle, J. (1993). *Ethnography and qualitative design in educational research.* New York: Academic.

Locke, D. C. (1992). *Increasing   multicultural   understanding: A comprehensive model.* Newbury Park, CA: SAGE.

Lubeck, S. (1996). Deconstructing "child development knowledge" and teacher preparation. *Early Childhood Research Quarterlty, 11* (2), 147-167.

Macias, J. (1987). The hidden curriculum of Papago teachers: American Indian strategies for mitigating cultural discontinuity in early schooling. In G. Spindler & L. Spindler (Eds.), *Interpretive ethnography at home and abroad.* Hillsdale, NJ: Lawrence Erlbaum Associates.

Mallory, B., & New, R. (Eds.). (1994). *Diversity and developmentally appropriate practices: Challenges for early childhood education.* New York: Teachers College Press.

Marshall, P. (1994). Four misconceptions about multicultural education that impede understanding, *Teacher Education, 16* (3), 19-27.

McAdoo, H. P. (Ed.). (1993). *Family ethnicity: Strength in diversity.* Newbury Park, CA: SAGE.

McAdoo, H. P. (Ed.). (1993). Family ethnicity: Strength in diversity. Newbury Park, CA: SAGE. Merseth, K. K. (1992). Cases for decision making in teacher education. In J. H. Shulman (Ed.), *Case methods in teacher education* (pp. 50-63). New York: Teacher College Press.

McCarthy, J. (1990). The content of early childhood teacher education programs: Pedagogy. In B. Spodek & O. Saracho (Eds.). *Early childhood teacher preparation: Yearbook in early childhood education* (pp. 82-101). Vol.1. New York: Teachers College Press.

McCracken, J. B. (1993). *Valuing diversity: The primary years.* Washington, DC: National Association for the Education of Young Children.

McLaren, P. (1989). *Life in schools.* New York: Longman.

Merriam, S. (1988). *Case study research in education*. San Francisco: Jossey-Bass.

Merseth, K. K. (1991). The early history of case-based instruction: Insights for teacher education today. *Journal of Teacher Education, 42* (4), 234-249.

Merseth, K. K. (1992). Cases for decision making in teacher education. In J.H. Shulman (Ed.), *Case methods in teacher education* (pp. 50-63). New York: Teacher College Press.

Miles, M., & Huberman, A. (1994). *Qualitative data analysis*. Newbury Park, CA: SAGE.

Min, P. G. (1988). The Korean American family. In C. H. Mindel, R. W. Habenstein, & R. Wright. (Eds). *Ethnic families in America: Patterns and variations* (3rd ed.). Englewood Cliffs, NJ: Prentice-Hall.

Mindel, C. H., Habenstein, R. W., & Wright, R. (1988). (Eds.) *Ethnic families in America: Patterns and variations* (3rd ed.). Englewood Cliffs, NJ: Prentice-Hall.

Mohatt, G. & Erickson, F. (1981). Cultural differences in teaching styles in an Odawa school: A sociolinguistic approach. In H. Trueba, G. Guthrie, & K. Au (Eds.), *Culture and the bilingual classroom: studies in classroom ethnography* (pp. 105-119). Rowley, MA: Newbury House.

Morine, G. (1976). *A study of teacher planning*. (tech. Rep. 76-3-1, Beginning Teacher Evaluation Study.) San Francisco: Far West Laboratory for Education Research and Development.(ERIC Document Reproduction Service No. ED 146160)

National Association for the Education of Young Children (1996). *Guidelines for preparation of early childhood professionals*. Washington, DC: Author.

National Council for Accreditation of Teacher Education. (1997). *Approved curriculum guidelines*. Washington, DC: Author.

National Council for Accreditation of Teacher Education. (1994). *Approved curriculum guidelines*. Washington, DC: Author.

National Council for Accreditation of Teacher Education. (1992). *Approved curriculum guidelines*. Washington, DC: Author.

National Council for Accreditation of Teacher Education. (1979). *Approved curriculum guidelines*. Washington, DC: Author.

Neely, A. M. (1986, May-June). Planning and problem solving in teacher education. *Journal of Teacher Education, 37* (3) 29-33.

New, R. (1994) Culture, child development, and developmentally appropriate practices. In B. L. Mallory & R. S. New (Eds.), *Diversity and developmentally appropriate practices: Challenge for early childhood education* (pp. 65-83). New York: Teachers College Press.

Nieto, S. (1992). *Affirming diversity: The sociopolitical context of multicultural education*. White Plains, NY: Longman.

Nissani, H. (1990). *Early childhood programs for language minority children. National Clearinghouse for Bilingual Education*. Occasional paper in bilingual education, No.2. (ERIC Document Reproduction Service No. ED 337033)

Nolan, J. F., & Francis, P. (1992). Changing perspectives in curriculum and instruction. In C. D. Glickman (Ed.), *Supervision in transition: 1992 Yearbook of the Association for Supervision and Curriculum Development* (pp. 44-60). Alexandria, VA: Association for Supervision and Curriculum Development.

Nolan, J. F., & Huber, T. (1989). Nurturing the reflective practitioner through instructional supervision: A review of the literature. *Journal of Curriculum and Supervision, 42* (2), 126-145.

Pajak, E. (1993). *Approaches to clinical supervision: Alternatives for improving instruction.* Norwood, MA: Christopher-Gordon.

Pan, H. (1994). Children's play in Taiwan. In J. Roopnarine, J. Johnson, & F. Hooper (Eds.), *Children's play in diverse cultures* (pp. 31-50). Albany, NY: SUNY Press.

Parten, M. (1933). Social play among preschool children. *Journal of Abnormal and Social Psychology, 28,* 136-147.

Patton, M. Q. (1990). *Qualitative evaluation and research methods.* (2nd ed.) Newbury Park, CA: SAGE.

Payne, C. (1977). A rationale for including multicultural education and its implementation in the daily lesson plan. *Journal of Research and Development in Education, 11* (1), 33-45.

Piaget, J. (1952). *The origins of intelligence in children* (Margaret Cook, Trens.) New York: International Universities Press. (Original French edition, 1936.)

Piaget, J., & Weil. A. M. (1951). The development in children of the ideal of the homeland and relations with other countries. *International Social Science Bulletin, 3,* 561-578.

Quintana, S. (1994). A model of ethnic perspective-taking ability applied to Mexican-American children and youth. *Journal of Intercultural Relations, 1* (18), 419-448.

Ramirez, R., & Castaneda, M. (1974). *Cultural democracy, bicognitive development and education.* New York: Academic.

Ramsey, P. (1987). *Teaching and learning in a diverse world: Multicultural education for young children.* New York: Teachers College Press.

Reagan, T. (1993). Educating the "reflective practitioner": The contribution of philosophy of education. *Journal of Research and Development in Education, 26* (4), 189-196.

Reiff, J., & Cannella, G. (1990, February). *Multicultural beliefs, personal beliefs, and conceptual level of preservice teachers*. Paper presented at the annual meeting of the Association of Teacher Educators, New Orleans, LA.

Renwick, G. W. (1974). Evaluation: Some practical guideline. In M. D. Push (Ed.), *Multicultural education: A cross-cultural training approach* (207-255). New York: Intercultural Press.

Rix, S. E. (Ed.). (1990). *The American women, 1990-1991: A status report*. New York: W.W. Norton.

Roopnarine, J. L., & Johnson, J. E. (1994). *Children's play in diverse cultures*. Albany, NY: SUNY Press.

Roopnarine, J., Hossain, Z., Gill, P., & Brophy, H. (1994). Play in the East Indian Context. In J. Roopnarine, J. Johnson, & F. Hooper (Eds.), *Children's play in diverse cultures* (pp. 9-30). Albany, NY: SUNY Press.

Roopnarine, J. L., Hooper, F. H., Ahmeduzzaman, M., & Pollack, B. (1993). Gentle play partners: Mother-child and father-child play in New Delhi, India, In K. MacDonald (Ed.). *Parents and children playing*. Albany, NY: SUNY Press.

Ross, D. D. (1989). Action research for preservice teachers: A description of why and how. *Peabody Journal of Education, 64* (3), 131-150.

Sanchez-Ayendez, M. (1988). The Puerto Rican American family. In C. H. Mindel, R. W. Habenstein, & R. Wright. (Eds.), *Ethnic families in America: Patterns and variations*. (3rd ed.) Englewood Cliffs, NJ: Prentice-Hall.

Schon, D. (1983). *The reflective practitioner: How professionals think in action*. New York: Basic Books.

Schultz, A. (1970). *On phenomenology and social relations*. Chicago, IL: University of Chicago Press.

Schwartzman, H. B. (1978). *Transformations: The anthropology of children's play*. New York: Plenum.

Schwartzman, H. B. (1983). *Child-structured play: A cross-cultural perspective*. In F. Manning (Ed.) The world of play (pp. 25-33). West Point, NY: Leisure Press.

Selman, R. (1980). *The growth of interpersonal understanding: Developmental and clinical analysis*. San Diego: Academic.

Selman, R., & Schultz, L. H. (1990). *Making a friend in youth; Developmental theory and pair therapy*. Chicago, IL: Chicago Press.

Shulman, J. H. (Ed.). (1992). *Case methods in teacher education*. New York: Columbia, Teachers College Press.

Shulman, L. S. (1987). Knowledge and teaching: Foundation of the new reform. *Harvard Educational Review, 57* (1), 1-22.

Shulman, J., & Mesa-Bains, A. (Eds.). (1994). *Diversity in the classroom: A casebook for teachers and teacher educators*. San Francisco, CA: Far West Laboratory.

Sizemore, B. (1979). The four M curriculum: A way to shape the future. *Journal of Negro Education, 47*, 341-356.

Sleeter, C. (1991). *Empowerment through multicultural education*. New York: SUNY Press.

Sleeter, C., & Grant, C. (1994). *Making choice for multicultural education: Five approaches to race, class, gender* (2nd ed.) New York: Macmillan.

Slonim, E. (1991). *Children, culture, and ethnicity: Evaluating and understanding the impact*. New York: Garland.

supervision of experienced teachers. *Curriculum Inquiry, 14,* 425-436.

Sparks-Langer, G., & Colton, A. (1991). Synthesis of research on teachers' reflective thinking. *Educational Leadership, 48* (6), 37-44.

Spodek, B., & Brown, P. (1993). Curriculum alternatives in early childhood education: A historical perspective. In B. Spodek (Ed.), *Handbook of research on the education of young children* (pp. 91-104). New York: Macmillan.

Staples, R. (1988). The Black American family. In C. H. Mindel, R. W. Habenstein, & R. Wright. (Eds.), *Ethnic families in America: Patterns and variations* (3rd ed.). Englewood Cliffs, NJ: Prentice-Hall.

Stewart, E., & Bennett, M. (1991). *American cultural patterns: A cross-cultural perspective.* Yarmouth, ME: Intercultural.

Stodolsky, S., & Lesser, G. (1967). Learning patterns in the disadvantaged. *Harvard Educational Review, 37,* 546-593.

Strauss, A., & Corbin, J. (1990). *Basics of qualitative research: Grounded theory procedures and techniques.* Newbury Park, CA: SAGE.

Swadener, B. B., & Miller-Marsh, M. (1993). *Antibias early childhood education: Toward a stronger teacher voice in research.* Eric Document Reproduction Series No. 362290.

Swadener, B., & Kessler, S. (Eds.). (1991). [Special Issue]. *Early Education and Development, 2* (2).

Szapocznik, J., & Hernandez, R. (1988). The Cuban American family. In C. H. Mindel, R. W. Habenstein, & R. Wright. (Eds). *Ethnic families in America: Patterns and variations* (3rd ed.), Englewood Cliffs, NJ: Prentice-Hall.

Takeuchi, M. (1994). Children's play in Japan. In J. Roopnarine, J. Johnson, & F. Hooper (Eds.), *Children's play in diverse cultures* (pp. 51-72). Albany, NY: SUNY Press.

Tharp, R. (1989). Psychocultural variables and constants: Effects on teaching and learning in schools. *American Psychologist, 44* (2), 349-359.

Thornburg, K., Hoffman, S., & Remeika, C. (1991). Youth at risk; society at risk. *The Elementary School Journal, 91* (3), 199-208.

Tran, T. V. (1988). The Vietnamese American family. In C. H. Mindel, R. W. Habenstein, & R. Wright. (Eds.), *Ethnic families in America: Patterns and variations* (3rd edition). Englewood Cliffs, NJ: Prentice-Hall.

Trent, W. (1991). Race and ethnicity in the teacher education curriculum. *Annual editions: Education 91/92* (pp. 147-150). Guilford, CT: Duskin.

Valli, L., & Taylor, N. (1988). Reflective teacher education: Preferred Characteristics. In H.C. Waxman, H. J. Freiberg, J. C. Vanghan, & M. Weil (Eds.), *Images of reflection in teacher education* (pp. 20-21). Reston, VA: Association for Teacher Educators.

van Manen, M. (1991). Reflectivity and the pedagogical moment: The normativity of pedagogical thinking and acting. *Journal of Curriculum Studies. 23* (6), 507-536.

van Manen, M. (1977). Linking ways of knowing with ways of being practical. *Curriculum Inquiry. 12* (6). 1-12.

Villegas, A. M. (1991). *Culturally responsive pedagogy for the 1990s and beyond. Trends and issues*. Eric Document Reproduction Series No. ED 339698.

Vogt, L., Jordan, C., & Tharp, R. C. (1987). Explaining school failure, producing school success: Two cases. *Ethnopology and Education*

Quarterly, 18 (4), 276-286.

Vygotsky, L. S. (1967). Play and its role in the mental development of the child. In M. Cole (Ed.), *Soviet Developmental Psychology* (pp. 76-99). White Plains, NY: M.E. Sharpe. (Original work published in 1966).

Vygotsky, L. S. (1967). Play and its role in the mental development of the child. *Soviet Psychology, 5* (3), 6-18.

Walsh, H. (1980). Introducing the young child to the social world. New York, NY: Macmillan.

Waxman, H. (1988). New images for reflecting about teacher education. In H. C. Waxman, H. J. Freiberg, J.C. Vanghan, & M. Weil (Eds.), *Images of reflection in teacher education* (pp. 5-6). Reston, VA: Association for Teacher Educators.

Wien, C. (1995). *Developmentally appropriate Practice in real life: Stories of teacher practical knowledge.* New York: Teachers College Press.

Wilkinson, D. (1993). Family ethnicity in America. In H.P.McAdoo (ed.) *Family ethnicity: Strength in diversity* (pp. 15-59). Newbury Park, CA: SAGE.

Williams, R. M., Jr. (1970). *American society: A sociological interpretation.* New York: Knopf.

Wong, M. G. (1988). The Chinese American family. In C. H. Mindel, R. W. Habenstein, & R. Wright. (Eds.), *Ethnic families in America: Patterns and variations* (3rd ed.). (pp. 230-257). Englewood Cliffs, NJ: Prentice-Hall.

Wortham, S. (1998). *Early childhood curriculum: Developmental basis for learning and teaching.* Upper Saddle River, NJ: Merrill.

York, S. (1991). *Roots and wings: Affirming culture in early childhood programs*. St. Paul, MN: Readleaf.

Zeichner, K. (1981-82). Reflective teaching and field-based experience in teacher education. *Interchange, 12*, 1-22.

Zeichner, K., & Liston, D. (1987). Teaching student teachers to reflect. *Harvard Educational Review, 57* (10), 23-48.

Author Index

Subject Index

A

analysis techniques, 105

anti-bias curriculum, 8, 11, 115, 118, 122

age appropriateness, 4

appropriate practice, 1, 2, 3

associate play, 16

attitude phase, 71

autobiographical self-awareness/self-examination, 31, 33, 99, 116, 126

axial coding, 113

B

Basic Components of DCAP, 10

C

case study approaches, 71

categorization, 108

characteristics of cross-cultural family ethnicity, 62

characteristics of multicultural pedagogical strategies, 9

child development, 72

child initiative free play, 129, 140

children's play, 15, 71, 138, 139

classroom conditions, 140

classroom culture, 140

clinical supervision, 86

clinical supervision cycle, 91

cognitive element, 81

complementary play, 17

conceptual focus, 80

contemporary cross-cultural perspectives on children's play, 19

cooperating teacher, 117, 127

cooperative play, 16

core categories, 113

critical element (of reflection), 81, 84

critical pedagogy, xiii, 5, 7, 8, 12, 41, 83, 140

critical reflection, 80, 85

critical thinking, 115

cross-cultural child development, 89

cultural appropriateness, 9

cultural compatibility, 9

cultural congruence, 9

cultural myopia, 31, 44

cultural relevance, 9

cultural responsiveness, 9

culturally congruent critical pedagogy, 76, 122, 131

culturally relevant, 5, 6, 131

D

developing (multiple/multiethnic) perspective-taking abilities, 44, 46

Developmentally and Culturally Appropriate Practice (DCAP), xii, xiii, 5, 8, 43

Developmentally Appropriate Practice (DAP), xi, 4, 5, 6, 7

dialectical focus, 80, 85

dialectical stage, 85

divergent questioning, 133, 135,
        137
divergent thinkers, 75

E
egocentrism, 44
emergent curriculum, 4
emerging cultures, 21
emerging patterns, 106
equal education, 37, 129
equal learning experience, 132,
        136
equal power sharing, 52
espoused platforms, 87
establishing readiness, 87, 95

F
fairness, 115, 116
field-based case studies, 135
field-based observations, 139
field-based questions, 34
field-dependent/independent, 42
field placement, 117, 127
formal lesson plan, 120, 139

G
gender roles, 125
generic lesson plans, 133, 138

H
hidden curriculum, 52
hidden environments, 2
hierarchical phenomenon, 78

I
ideological constraints, 85
impact focus, 80

individual appropriateness, 4
individual differences, 130, 131,
        132, 133
individualism, 15
inner dialogue, 81, 82, 83
inquiry-oriented approach, 85
inquiry-oriented reflective
supervision, xv, 75
inquiry-oriented reflective
teaching, 86
instrumental focus, 80
inter-ethnic relations, 42
internal cues, 123
intersubjectivity, 94
intra-ethnic phenomena, 42
interpersonal negotiation
strategies, 46

L
learning styles, 3, 43
lesson planning, 88, 90, 100, 136
lived curriculum, 4

M
mental lesson planning, 90, 101,
        131
mitigating cultural discontinuity,
        9
multiple and multiethnic
perspective-taking, 29,38, 41,
        124
multiple perspectives, 83
multiple perspective-takers, 7
multiple power sharing, 52

N
narrative element, 81, 83
National Association for the